Rugby!
Be the best 'You' you can be!

- Prologue

Rugby Union is widely considered a game of intelligence,
strategy, teamwork and strength, both physical and mental.
These are the principles a Rugby player needs to develop in
order to succeed in the sport. If you have the opportunity to
watch a Rugby training session, which can be achieved from
the comfort of your own sofa, you will see the time that is
spent on the intellect of the Rugby player. These are not just
opportunities for the Coaches to teach new plays or develop
new skills, this is to develop the mind of the Rugby player to
increase their understanding of the psychology of the game,
understand their opponent and their own team. It is vital
that the Rugby player understands the abilities of those
around them, both physical and mental. It is also important
for them to understand, as much as possible, the
oppositions` abilities, both mental and physical. Not being
prepared for a game means not knowing your team or your
opponent and that will lead to defeat. There is no excuse for
the Rugby player that comes to the game physically
unprepared. They can't keep up with the game and that leads
to the defensive line having gaps and weak areas for the

opponents to get through. Likewise, in attack, the player who is unprepared physically is not able to keep up with the ball, finding themselves out of position for plays, not breaking through Tackles, not having the constant pace throughout the game to carry the ball past the Gain line. The physically unprepared Rugby player will inevitably not be able to fulfil their role in their position. This will result in loss of structure in the team, loss of ground to the opposition, loss of ball and eventually loss of the game. The physically unprepared player will become a liability for their team, finding themselves substituted, dropped, or worst of all, injured. This can be career ending and there is no one that will help because there is no excuse for not preparing.

The same is true for the mentally unprepared Rugby player. The saying is true, this is a game of intelligence. The mentally unprepared Rugby player will have no idea how their team can perform. I'm not just talking about understanding the basic position and rules of the game, I'm talking about understanding the strengths, weaknesses and mental abilities of the team and their opposition. We have all enjoyed watching sport and seen, so many times, the greats of the sporting world, brilliant in their field, beautiful to behold, how they command their position and their opposition. With grace and style, they dominate and destroy with ease and at will but some of the greatest also seem to have an inability to fully control their emotions. John McEnroe famously lost his cool in 1981, with a Wimbledon umpire, leaving a generation screaming at each other every time something went wrong, "You cannot be serious"! Paul Gascoigne broke down when he received a yellow card meaning he would miss the final in the 1990 world cup after sliding into a tackle. Mike Tyson bit off part of Evander Holyfield's ear in their fight in 1997. And there are oh so many times Rugby players have resorted to fighting during the game. Leicester Centre, Manu Tuilagi received a five week ban for punching Northampton's Chris Ashton in a Premiership game in 2011, landing 3 punches that would rival any boxer. These sports stars were all at the top of their game but still had a lack of mental control. It is understood that when you are at such a high level in any profession there is a lot of pressure. In sports they are playing at their peak with all others trying to knock them off the top spot and the prepared player can get under the skin of their opposition, pressing the buttons that cause them to lose control and ultimately the game. The mentally unprepared Rugby player is as much a liability to their team as the physically unprepared. In order to be the best, a Rugby player needs to be prepared in body and mind. Not only having complete control of themselves but also an ability to influence the opposition to gain an advantage over them. Self-control is the key to victory!

When I started in business, I understood it was important to grow a great company, so I tried to organise my company in a way that suited me. I was the boss, the leader, so it was

3

important I took a direction with the company that worked for me. I thought I could get anyone to do what I wanted for the sakes of my business by employment and a fair pay cheque. I quickly realised that there are so many different reasons people go to work and my success and benefits is not one of them! In fact, there is only one person in the history of the world that truly wants me to be a success and receive all the benefits that come with it, and that's me!

Reasons for going to work are personal to each of us. That doesn't mean not sharing them with others, just that they don't mean much to anyone but ourselves. The most common is to pay the bills, but that's usually a very necessary reason. Underneath that there are reasons like; social interaction, enjoyment, health, satisfying curiosity, fulfilling dreams, to get away from the other half and so on. I have not met anyone that says, "it is to give my boss the success and benefits they want". This means that you cannot rely on pay alone to incentivise your company. There are so many reasons that someone will work hard to give you the success and benefits that come with it, you just have to figure out what motivates them.

When I became a Dad, I found myself in a similar predicament. As much as I love my children and want the best for them, they seemed to have other ideas. Getting them to bed at a reasonable hour was, as far as I felt, important for them so that they would wake in the morning refreshed and full of life and energy to grow, learn and become strong intelligent adults. This, however, was not how they saw it.

I needed to understand how I could motivate my company and my children. I started to read books on motivation, leadership and business. I learned that there were so many specialists and techniques that all referred to "building the team". They would use expressions from sports but would not draw any lessons from the sport mentioned. I also found myself using expressions and analogies from sport to get my children to understand things. I realised then that in all the leadership, motivation, self-help and management books and articles I had been reading, none of them were more helpful than an actual sports team. I realised that to build a great company you need a great team, no matter how big or small, so why not study the greatest teams? How are they motivated, how are they lead, how do they prepare and why am I not learning from them?

I know this book is titled "Rugby!", but the principles are the same in any, and I mean any, sport. Even if the sport is an individual sport like Snooker, they have a team around them, training them, preparing them. Boxing isn't considered a team sport, but I have never seen a Boxer that sits in their corner alone. All sports have the team mentality, spirit and philosophy. So why are we not reading sports books instead of leadership books when all the lessons are there in front of us each time we watch our favourite team.

The lessons in this book are not new, they have been used in analogies and phrases have been coined throughout the years to teach or explain. I am just illustrating how looking at life through the perspective of the Rugby Union team has helped me understand and prepare myself in business and in my private life. How it makes us all a great team, however, other sports are available.

Looking through Rugby's history brings up so many examples of great passes, from the backhand offload to the long pass to the Wings. From the fast flat accurate pass to the quick hands literally tapping the ball on to the next player. Above all, it is the pass that opens up play and releases a player to make valuable gains on the field. That is how a pass is judged by the players and that is what counts!

All players love to have a go at a fancy pass. In grass roots Rugby the eager young players love to try to spin the ball out of the back of the hand, emulating their heroes. Showing off to their mates, the hopelessly inaccurate and wayward attempt at a pass they saw on the TV or at the game during the weekend. And, if we are all honest, we all do the same whether we are Rugby players or not.

The truth is, whenever we see anything that we think is amazing, incredible, cool, awesome, we have a desire within ourselves to wish we could do it. As we grow older, we resist the urge to attempt to try, for fear of ridicule and embarrassment. I wish I was a kid again just to try the ridiculous things without fear of looking stupid.

In 2018 Aaron Smith was considered the greatest Scrum Half in Rugby Union. He was considered to have the most reliable pass that provided flat, wide, lightning-quick ball. His ability to clear the ball so quickly and accurately provided a platform for the All Blacks to play at a ferocious pace.

He used to practice when he was young by passing a ball to a wheelie bin with a sticker on it. If the pass was right, the ball would bounce straight back off the bin into his hands, however, if the pass was off centre, low, high, uncontrolled or not powerful enough, then it would bounce off across the yard with him having to chase after it. This constant practice and attention to accuracy has given him the opportunity to play in arguably the greatest team in the world.

I am not about to suggest one pass in history that I think is the perfect pass. There are so many great passes that have been recorded for so many different reasons. However, if you research "The greatest passes of all time" the results are almost all back-hand offloads and over the top backhand throws.

So how do you qualify the perfect pass? I know that when watching Rugby, we all love to see showboating, flair and audacious skill, if it comes off. If we don't see enough of this, as fans, we feel the game was flat or lacked pace and excitement, after all we want to be entertained. The problem lies when the showboating, flair and audacious skill does not come off. This is when the fan becomes an expert in the basics. We shout at the player in disgust, asking why they would even try such a reckless attempt rather than picking the simple pass, going through the hands, working the ball out wide and sticking to the basics. There is a fine line between the greatest pass and the worst.

I suppose then that there is a difference between the perfect pass and the greatest pass. The perfect pass is nothing to do with flair or audacious skill. If you ask any professional sports man or woman how to create the perfect pass, move, hit, run or position in their chosen sport they would say that the basics need to be right. Practice the basics and you will always be able to do it right. Listening to professional Rugby players talk about the pass, they will always say they want a good, clean, flat pass that they can run onto without losing momentum. This gives the receiver the opportunity to be balanced, using the speed and position they have generated to gain territory on the field. The perfect pass is so much more than the ball leaving one player's hands and being caught by another. No matter how powerful or how accurate the pass, it needs to be to the right player at the right time.

Danny Cipriani to Charlie Sharples for Gloucester against Northampton Saints in the Gallagher Premiership.

Around half an hour into the game, Gloucester had the put in for the Scrum in the Northampton 22 and the ball was controlled at the back by Ben Morgan (Number Eight). Callum Braley (Scrum Half) backs off from the back of the Scrum as Morgan picks the ball and passes out to Braley. Billy Twelvetrees (Centre) makes a dummy run drawing in an opposition player. Braley passes on to the hands of Danny

Cipriani in the middle of the pitch. With Jason Woodward (Full Back) and Charlie Sharples (Wing) to his right-hand side and with two opposition players in defence against them, Cipriani straightened his run. With Woodward running a direct line between the two defenders, the defenders stepped in field towards him. Sharples started his run from deep as Cipriani lofted a magnificent pass over the top of the Full Back to his right, directly into the path of the speeding Winger. Sharples caught the pass on the run and his speed and momentum carried him passed the Northampton defenders over for an easy Try.

The commentators all raved about the "magic" that Cipriani weaved into the Gloucester game and the "magnificent pass" that created the easy over for Sharples. There was no doubt that the pass was very accurate and timed to perfection however, analysing the play that led to the pass showed that Cipriani's part in the move was reliant on all involved.

From the Scrum all players knew where their teammates were. The ball was released with urgency and accuracy. As the ball was passed through the hands, Cipriani positioned himself and the ball was delivered to him with precision. If the delivery had been off, then Cipriani would have had to adjust his position to catch the ball putting him potentially off balance and out of position, this would have made the pass to the Wing much more difficult. When the ball was received by Cipriani, he had the position and balance to execute the pass with power, accuracy and timing. During this, Sharples had started his run. Seeing the space and the position of Cipriani he timed his run so that he would reach speed at the position he anticipated Cipriani would pass the ball. If his timing had been too early, then he would have had to slow his run to receive the pass leaving him with no speed or momentum to carry himself over the line. If his run had been too late then the ball would have bounced in front of him and, at best, gone into touch. Likewise, if Cipriani's pass had been behind or in front of Sharples position then the outcome would have been similar.

Looking at this play, the "magnificent pass" by Cipriani was not just a great pass but it relied on all the other elements of the play to be perfect. If Sharples timing had been off then there would be no punditry about the "magic weaved" or the "magnificent pass", there may have been comments about the vision but if a pass is not caught, is there a pass at all?

I had been working for a couple of guys that I had worked with in the past and knew well. They were trying to grow their company and had asked me to help. I was given the title of Operations Manager which I was happy with, I knew the industry well and had complete confidence in my abilities to fulfil the role. Things were going well until the Production Manager decided to quit. The Directors were reluctant to replace him, preferring to promote within to cut costs. I felt that there weren't any current employees who were experienced enough to fulfil the role and suggested that replacing him would be worth the cost. After a few days they agreed that there weren't any operatives they could promote. I thought they had made the right decision but was not prepared for what came next. They told me that 'Operations Manager' now included `Production`! I had my hands full and lacked the capability to take on more responsibilities, but as quickly as that, they passed me all the responsibility and added workload. I was not prepared for this pass! Over the next year I took it by the fingertips and stumbled along trying to keep going, trying to keep my feet underneath me, trying not to drop the ball. These guys prided themselves on being good delegators, they thought they understood their team. They had passed me a ball that I was not ready for and they should have realised that even though I took the pass by the fingertips, I was not in a position to, or had support for, the extra workload that came with the position. I was carrying out both jobs, but I wasn't doing either of them as wholeheartedly as I wanted. I have always given 100% but when you need to be in two positions at the same time you are unable to give 100% to both. The company growth slowed. Jobs were getting done but the efficiency decreased. The Directors, however, were still processing new work at the pace they had been when we were growing, and running efficiently, and this started to backlog. Customers were becoming irritated and so was I. The Directors eventually realised what was happening and they employed a Production Manager, but it was too late.

I learned then that you cannot pass over responsibility to just anyone. I thought I could do it for the sake of the team, but I was not prepared. I was not in the right place on the field and I had received a "Hospital Pass". Hospital Pass - describes a pass that subjects the recipient to heavy contact, usually unavoidable, from an opposing player. The expression implies that the recipient of the pass could end up in hospital. We have all seen the perfectly timed Tackle when a player anticipates a pass and starts their run towards their opponent. Their opponent then receives a pass that leaves them completely exposed, usually reaching for a ball that has been passed right over their head or on their toes, just as the tackling player hits. The receiving player has no time to avoid the Tackle or even bring their hands down to protect themselves. They are completely exposed to the massive impact of the Tackle. The stadium rumbles with the sound of all supporters from both sides as they, in unison, express "OOOOOOOOHHH" for the player. The Tackle usually is a good clean Tackle, well timed and perfectly executed. However, if the player had been in position and the pass had been accurate and fast then the player would have had the ability to react, or at the very least have their hands and arms ready for some protection. The player takes a while to recover from the Hospital Pass. Sometimes they won't recover for the rest of the game. Not just a physical recovery, the player is left feeling mentally bruised. Every Tackle they receive from now on they will want to protect themselves more. It knocks their confidence and often, even if they have not been injured, they will be substituted to recover.

Life is all about the pass! When you ask anyone to do anything make sure they are ready, willing and able to do it. Likewise, they may even be asking but if you are not ready or prepared to hand it over you will not pass it over well and that will make it harder for them. If they are not ready or prepared to receive the pass you must wait or find an alternative. If you have the ball in a game and a player is calling but they have two defenders bearing down on them look for an alternative, you will only be playing them into trouble if you pass them the ball. You will not help the team get to the try line if you pass the ball to someone who is not in the correct position to carry it. You may be in a position where you have the pressure of two defenders in front of you but you or your team are out of position. If there are no easy passes to make to your team then you are better to go into the Tackle, protect the ball, go to ground and wait for support, reset and recycle the ball and go again.

Life is a team sport and no matter how big your team is, even if you say you are a "one-man band" you will still need to pass or receive the ball. It might be from a supplier, a colleague, or a client, it all requires timing, precision and preparation. Whether you are a family member, or single, you will still interact with others you like, love, loathe or tolerate. Be sure you consider whether you have done your best by them and yourself. Being a good delegator has nothing to do with handing over responsibility for something, being a good delegator is about taking responsibility for how you hand it over. Whether at work or in your private life, understand your abilities and position, your team's abilities and their positions and you will understand how to be a good delegator. Do not just fling over a task to anyone just to make your life easier, thinking you have delegated responsibility of it. The responsibility remains with you, all you have done is play someone on your team into trouble and now your team is on the back foot and in danger of losing. You also may find that you aren't a team for long.

When I was young, I never dreamed of being a professional Rugby player. There was no place for that sort of thinking in my life. Struggling academically at school, I had been told to get a manual labour profession and make sure I had skills that would help me throughout the long life ahead. "Get yourself a trade and you will always have work". This sort of teaching was, and is still, commonplace so I have no regrets in not thinking that Rugby, Football, Cricket or any other sport could have been a profession when I was young.

The heroes of my youth, Sir Bill Beaumont (then just Bill Beaumont), Steve Davis, Kenny Dalglish and so many more, were sportsmen! This was something that never ever entered my world as something that could provide a future or income for real life. I didn't know anybody that made a living from sports in the real world. My uncle had a friend that knew the great Ian `Beefy` Botham, but even that disconnection was too great to put it into any sort of reality. Emulating these giants of my youth was as attainable as the superhero in the comics. I was `Beefy` when we played Cricket, I was Will Carling when we played Rugby, I was Ian Rush when we played Football and I was Daley Thompson at all other times, but there was never a time when I thought I could actually become one of them. They were as real as the

17

comics, and my imagination and dreams were swept away by the reality of life in the same profession for 25 years.

As we grow, we adapt to the responsibilities of life that start to come thick and fast once we leave school. Work, car, partners, mortgage, bills and then the big one, parenthood! With each responsibility we find ourselves grounded a little bit more. The dreams fade and we start to find ourselves hoping that our offspring might find life a little easier if we could just impart some of our knowledge on to them. We see them dreaming that they will be the next Maggie Alphonsi or Jonathan Joseph. We indulge them with grass roots sports but then find ourselves suggesting, as they go through school, that they should be starting to think about a career. The talk moves on to trades, professions, employment and less and less about becoming a Rugby player. Inadvertently, we start to wash away their dreams with realities, just like ours had been.

Don't get me wrong, I know that there are lots of children who have no desire to become sports professionals, but they all grow up with dreams of becoming something that they see as great, and as they grow we start to put pressure on them to decide on a path that leads to security and stability. Slowly but surely those childhood dreams fade away.

When I became a Dad, I realised that all the importance of life was there in my hands. I was responsible for this new life, to help them grow, learn, interact safely in their surroundings, so that one day they would be able to stand on their own two feet. I felt that I had only just about managed to stand on my own two feet and now I was responsible for another. Whether you are a parent, husband, wife, partner in life or business, daughter, son or any sort of friend, you have a responsibility for someone and that means being able to help in whatever capacity you can.

As time went on, I stumbled through, trying to do my best by my family, and as my children grew, I realised that it was becoming more and more difficult to give answers to a son who had so many questions about life and his surroundings. Even though access to the internet and all its amazing facts is in our pockets at all times, trying to find the answer to `why little Johnny at school would not let him play with them` seemed impossible to find. Trying to understand what goes on in the playground is nothing short of a mystery. Seeing that my son was trying to learn and understand the wonderful, and often confusing, world around him, to try to interact, fit in with the other lives running around the playground. It was no surprise that the questions came thick and fast. I came to dread the word that flowed so slowly and lazily out of his mouth, "Daaaaaad?". It was always followed with something that made me wish I had applied myself at school and chosen psychology as a profession instead.

It was not long before he got interested in Rugby. Fantastic!!! Finally, something I understood, and the questions about

Rugby were easy. This seemed like a great relief after the difficult questions regarding the complex psychology of the playground, however, this relief was short lived. Once he started to get more involved in his local Rugby club and got to grips with the beautiful game the questions became answers, it seemed there was nothing he didn't know about Rugby. I should not have complained because when the questions about Rugby stopped and turned into answers, the questions about life returned, but this time they were even more complicated than ever.

Realising it was too late to return to school to get that psychology qualification I looked for some other way to help explain the complexities of life. Something I knew and he would understand. Something I understood and he would know. When asked why the kids at school didn't want him to play with them, this time I had the answer. "You know the kid at Rugby that gets the ball and doesn't pass but just plays his own game?" "Yeah! Nobody wants to pass to him coz he just won't pass the ball." "Okay... well that's why the kids at school don't want you to play... you have to play their game if you want to play... it's not all about you in a Rugby team, you can't just play your game, you have to pass the ball!"

The questions came and I started to find so many answers in Rugby, until we decided between us that life... the way we live, the way we interact, the way we work and the way we play, is just like a game of Rugby, a team! Whether we are striving for victory, battling against an opposition trying to be victorious over us, developing ourselves or just enjoying the game, Rugby is life!

Talking to my son about Rugby, and how it helps us understand life, answering questions using Rugby as a comparison for the circumstances he found himself in, I realised that helping him was having a profound effect on how I was performing at work. I realised that I was starting to see things at work in the same way I was explaining them with him. I was starting to work more as a team player, looking after, and supporting, my team at work. Also, at home we were all picking up on the ethos I was trying to instil in him of being his team. We were sharing tasks to help each other out because that's what you do in a Rugby team, you support. If one player is struggling to perform their part in the team then the others will rally around and support so that the team works together to succeed. This was starting to mean that things that were normally a chore were starting to be done without a fuss. After all, in a team there is always a need to do the hard graft to free up the players to run in the try. Everyone benefits when you work hard for the team.

It started to dawn on me that this way of thinking would help me if I applied it in business. We all hate to work with the person who is not a team player, insisting on doing it their way, not helping or working with you. We all know what it is like when you are left with the lion's share of the work and everyone goes home when they have finished their part. Nobody on a Rugby pitch leaves until the job is done and if you are struggling because you are left holding the ball with a mammoth task ahead of you, you can guarantee you will have the whole team behind you following you up to help.

The pass is one of those things that can make or break success. Just think about the processes of the pass explained in the previous chapter. Think of a particular part of your job at work and think of this as `the ball`. It can be a small, individual process or a complete project that you are working on. Before you receive the ball, you need to make sure you are in position and ready to receive it. If, for any reason, you are not ready to receive the ball, there is a good chance you will drop it. If you are not in position you are better to let your teammate know you are not ready to receive the ball so that they can keep it safe until you are ready or pass it to another teammate that is ready. This is not a failure. It is only a failure if you try to receive the ball and knock on because you were not ready and didn't let your team know. Your team will not thank you for being out of position and not telling them. They will however appreciate you giving them the chance to pick another option that will help keep control.

Likewise, when you are in control of the ball and looking to pass, it is not enough for you to have done your part and pass the ball without consideration to the receiver. You must consider their position, their ability, the chance of them receiving the ball and controlling it. You cannot just fling a pass with no control, you must make sure it is swift, direct, and perfectly weighted so that the receiver can take it with as little adjustments to enable them to keep the momentum going. It is all about the pass!

I know it is not new to say teamwork is how we achieve success, and I know that all sports, including individual sports like Golf, Tennis, Snooker etc. all have a team mentality that can be used to apply these principles, but for me... Rugby is life!

This way of thinking is not limited to Rugby, or indeed Business, but can be applied in all parts of our life. The chores at home became easier when everyone realised that if you want to get to the game and there is a job someone needs to get done beforehand, if the team work together, the job can be done in no time, leaving all the time needed to get to the game.

My son started to interact well at school and Rugby, but he wasn't getting his homework completed and his teachers were concerned his grades would be affected. I said to him, "I know you want to play Rugby this weekend, but you are having to do a lot of homework and it's taking a long time. You are struggling to get it done and that means you are having to do more at school and home to keep up. I don't want you to miss Rugby, but your schoolwork is important. Remember when you wanted to become a Centre how you had to focus, learn and work hard at training and, with extra hard work and practice, you started to find it easier to play that position? Well, you just need to apply that same focus and hard work to school. You are in danger of not being prepared and that means you will drop the ball. look at school like it's Rugby training. Work hard and prepare for the game, otherwise you will not be able to play your position because you will have so much extra homework to complete". He started to get his homework completed more quickly, with more focus and accuracy, so as not to have to repeat it. His grades improved; he was even put up a class in some of his subjects. Subsequently he had got into the right position and prepared himself for his Rugby. He never missed a training session and always had his homework completed.

At work I was finding that the "Rugby is Life" mentality was having a positive effect on me and my business. I was not thinking about me and my goals anymore. I was realising that the guys who were working for us were not me. I was a typical Second Row No.5., I used power and strength to make things happen and wanted everyone to have the same mentality and do things the way I did them. Have you ever seen a Rugby team made up solely of Second Row's? Can you even imagine it, the thought sends shivers down my spine, a team of powerful and strong but heavy, slow and cumbersome players that struggle to pass or kick a ball? I remember as a player the ball once bobbled to my feet from a Tackle and as I picked it up, I was on our 22-metre line. I looked up and there was nobody in front of me just an open pitch. It was a fluke of course, nobody had anticipated the ball landing at my feet, least of all me, but I started my run for glory. I ran and ran like the wind and before I got to the halfway line I thought "shit, there is no way in hell I am going to make the try line, please somebody Tackle me, put me out of my misery, where are the Backs? This is their job not mine, what am I doing here?" Of course, it didn't take long for someone to chase me down. I realised that I could not expect everyone at work to be like me. We needed different skills on the team and for them to do things their way, not mine. We needed some Forwards to do the heavy gritty work, but we also needed some Backs that were quick, agile and accurate as well, and they all needed to prepare and train differently. They all needed different equipment to go with their different skills and, more importantly, they all had a different way of doing things, but the same mentality and goal... the Try!

A wonderous scene witnessed by mankind since the
beginning of time when the first odd-shaped ball was kicked
along the earth. The bounce has been a dance of beauty and
intrigue between the player and the nature and power of the
cosmos. The Centre receives the responsibility of the game
and sees space behind the defence as if it were a green
pasture of peace and tranquillity and, as if in harmony and
spiritual connection with the Wing, he drops the ball to his
feet and with total control sends the ball firmly on its journey
with the laces of his shining black boots. Like an eagle after
its prey the Wing takes flight. Through the defence he jinks
and weaves, his eyes fixed on the ball as it skips along the
hallowed turf. The Wing breaks through the line of defence
and finds himself being chased down by the enemy that is
now behind him. He won't take his eyes of the prize as he
prays, along with his army of troops and the crowds who
support them screaming their prayers to the earth on which
they do battle, that the spirits of the ball will be favourable to
his cause and lift it from the earth into his arms. As if the
spirits heard, the ball rises from the green flames it has
skipped along for so long, lifted by the hopes and dreams of
all who look on, into the willing arms of the flying Wing. He
wraps his powerful arms around the ball as the eagle closes
its wings over its prey to claim it, and time stops. He ceases

his agonising charge and finds peace in the moment of unity between player and ball. All hearts stop and all hold their breath in a moment of anticipation and wonder as the Wing, lifted on the same hopes and dreams, floats through the air. Not flying any more but gliding on a cushion of majesty that carries him over the line and rests him back down onto the green flames from which the ball rose into his arms. As if ordained by the spirits of the ball, the ballet comes to an end as rapture erupts from all who fight with him to tumultuous applause.

Or it was just a lucky bounce!!!

The beauty of the lucky bounce is a wonder. Many arguments have been made over luck and many games won too. The grubber is a kick that is used so often but is so unpredictable. Yes, there is a skill in getting the ball to turn over on its end along the grass but ultimately whether the ball bounces up or not is down to luck. What we can be sure of is it will eventually stop.

I have always tried to explain to my son that you make your own luck. This is a concept that I do not often explain to people I speak to as there is a propensity to get into a discussion of fate, destiny, if it's meant to be it will be. This is not what I mean when I say you make your own luck.

For example, I often hear people say, "that's just bad luck". I understand there is no control over certain events in life and that bad things happen as well as good things. Control is not what I am talking about when I say you make your own luck either.

Look at the time in your life when you thought that there was nothing else you could do. You had tried everything and just couldn`t fulfil the thing you were trying for or to do. You were about to give up and, just as luck would have it, something came up. Or you heard about something, or you found it underneath the coffee table when you bent down to pick up the glasses you just dropped.

This kind of luck doesn`t happen unless you are looking for it. If something is on your mind, you are alerted to things that relate to it. For example, you have seen a new car you would like to buy. It is just right for you and on top of it all it looks great. Then you start to see them out and about on the road. You hadn't noticed them before but now you see them regularly. This is because your subconscious has been emotionalised to this particular thing. Emotions stimulate your senses making you more alert to the subject matter and therefore your senses alert you when they pick up anything relating to it.

The time in your life when you were just about to give up, at your wits end, tearing your hair out, is the time when you are at your most emotional and therefore your senses are most alert. You catch a conversation between someone or remember something that was said that can give you access to the answer. Catching sight of something when you are out, or the flash of inspiration that comes into your mind whilst talking about your struggle, is a result of your senses working overtime.

You have control over your conscious mind. You decide what you think about and do in a day, but your subconscious is not under your control. However, it will respond to your emotion. We don't decide what we dream about at night, but we can influence whether the dreams are good or bad by the emotions we feel when we are falling asleep. If you watch a horror movie before bed, and it has had an emotional impact on you, there is a good chance you will have a nightmare, however, if you have spent an evening on a date with someone you are falling in love with, and the evening was as amazing as you had hoped, then you will probably have happy and peaceful dreams.

Your emotionalised senses will help provide you with `luck`, or will alert you to the many opportunities that come into your periphery on a daily basis that ordinarily you would not see. In this state of emotion your senses will help you without you knowing and therefore most people only see this as luck.

The other way you make your own luck is being in the place where the opportunity or thing you seek is. This is just as true for bad luck as good. Many extreme sports people have had serious injuries or lost lives to bad luck. They have been brilliant at what they do, experts, world class but something failed, the elements changed, or the unexpected happened. All things in life carry a degree of risk. Some far more than others and some people can't get enough of the adrenaline rush from facing the danger and beating it. I must admit to enjoying that rush myself however, if I didn't put myself in the situation that carries such a degree of risk, then when that thing failed or when the elements changed or the unexpected happened, I would not be in that danger situation and therefore the `bad luck` would not happen to me. Good luck telling a base jumper that the risk is too great and to quit... it's not in their makeup. They would say "it is not life if it is not adrenaline fuelled", and happily face the risk, bad luck or not.

Good luck is no different. Many times, people say, "It was just the right place at the right time". I can say it of myself many times in my life and I'm sure you can too. If you are a business person, then you make sure everyone knows your business. At a conference you might meet someone that can add value to your business, or you can get business from. We don't think of this as luck because we are there for that exact reason. However, if you weren't there it would not have happened. Some of us met our husbands, wives, partners by a chance meeting when socialising with friends. Some of us got a job just talking to people in that business. If you put yourself in the place where opportunity might be then you have a chance of receiving it.

Gary Player the South African golfing legend was once asked about being lucky and he replied, "Well, the harder I practice the luckier I get!".

The Roman philosopher Seneca, who lived between 4 BC and 65 AD, stated that Luck is what happens when preparation meets opportunity.

As the ball is kicked through by the Centre, it bobbles and skips along the grass. The Wing reacts and makes chase. they don't know how the ball will run, if it will bounce up for them, if it will skip into touch or if it will bounce left or right. All they know is that if they are not there and the opportunity comes then they will not get the lucky bounce. There is no lucky bounce if no one is there to catch it. We watch a kicking game today and so many times we see an up and under chased down by the Full Back that bounces off the turf so perfectly into their hands that it is like a higher power had put it there. However, when the player never gets there because the kick was long or the player was prevented from getting close, we never think `that ball bounced so perfectly that it could have been perfect for them`, we just see the ball bounce.

When starting a business or starting out on your own you have put yourself in a position to take any opportunity relating to that business that comes along. Successful entrepreneurs will tell you that the most important thing when thinking about starting a business is, JUST START! They´

will regale you with stories of how they had no idea what they were doing when they started out, but they learnt on the way and more and more opportunities come along when you decide to `do`!

I was chatting with a friend and I listened as he told me about an old colleague of his that was so lucky. He told me that he had been living with his wife and when they got divorced, he bought his ex-wife out of their property. He said that he then had a distant relative who died, leaving a very old but very large property to their family. He mortgaged himself to the max and bought the property from his relatives and renovated it. As the market was on the up, he found himself sitting on a profit of a few hundred thousand pounds. He then bought another property with the profit and did the same and now, a number of properties later, lives by the sea in a multi-million-pound house and drives a very expensive sports car. When I asked why his friend was lucky, he said that his friend was lucky to have been able to buy his first house, and then his relatives house, and make so much money on it. I said to him that his friend probably didn't feel lucky when his marriage finished. Also, he probably didn't feel lucky when he started to pile money into the old property hoping that he could complete it before it became unprofitable. He also probably didn't feel lucky when he spent all the money he had worked so hard for, renovating the old property, on another property that he hoped to make a profit on.

You don't know how the ball will bounce, but it will never bounce for you if you are not there to take it. Chase hard, be prepared and when opportunity pops up, take it with both hands and go for the try line.

Make your own luck!

There are so many opportunities in front of us every day, the only difference between us is, the lucky ones saw the opportunity and took it. The unlucky ones decided that there was no opportunity because the risk was too great, or the timing was wrong or the difficulty was too much to undertake, or it's just too good to be true, or, or, or, excuse, excuse, excuse. If you are prepared, then when the opportunity comes along it seems more like fate then opportunity. Instead of, you can't afford to, the reality should be, can you afford not to. When I started out in business, I found myself in fear of failure, and when I found myself in a position where I was thinking that work was not coming, something always came along in the nick of time. Your emotions enhance your senses to be more alert to the opportunities or actions that seemed previously absent. The reality is that you spend a long time preparing yourself so when the opportunity comes along you are ready to take it. You are, however, not aware of when or from where these will come and so the opportunities seem to take forever.

Start the ball rolling and put yourself in position to receive the opportunity if and when it arises. Chase the grubber and the high ball, make the run, put the work in and take that lucky bounce when it comes.

"Make your own luck!"

Firstly, the Scrum is far more intricate than it appears on the surface. The games that go on beneath the mass is quite often unseen. The way the Scrum is controlled and worked is a well-practiced technical piece of skill. The Scrum is a measure of power, strength, control and stability with the pack working in complete harmony to overpower the opposition.

Although rarely does the team that has the `put-in` not retain the ball, the Scrum can be disrupted so completely that the opposing team can gain the upper hand. After the ball has been released, the attacking team can be put under pressure to kick away possession or give up metres in order to regroup. The Scrummaging can also be so successful that the opposition can be caused to give away a penalty because of instability in one form or another. Ultimately, with teamwork, effort and coordination, control can be over-turned, and the opposing pack can gain possession of the ball.

The Scrum is formed by eight players in three rows, and without the players working in harmony the Scrum will breakdown.

The front row is where the battling happens, with the Props and Hookers doing their best to psychologically master their opposite numbers. They stand as wide as possible to look like they are immovable. Their faces snarling with taped heads and gumshields that are designed to make them as imposing looking as possible. They crouch… bind… and set… with as much force as possible over a few inches of movement. They then begin the battle, forcing their heads up into the chest of their opponents, pulling and pushing the binding arms of their opposite numbers using every tactic to disrupt and unbalance. The battle for the ball is really not contested and, although the ball should be put into the Scrum straight, it very rarely is. This is the advantage of the Scrum `put-in`. You have control over when and how the ball is presented into the battle. The Hooker with one quick movement hooks the ball back onto his side of the Scrum.

The Second Row is made up of two monsters of the game called The Locks. Upon these two, the Scrum is built, the rock, the foundation, the Locks. These two bring together the power and strength of the pack. Binding onto the thighs of the two Props with one arm and binding around each other with the other arm, they lock the pack together and provide stability and power to drive the pack forwards.

The third row is made up of the two Flankers who are adding power to the Scrum whilst keeping it on the right path. They are also keeping an eye on the play outside of the Scrum, anticipating the move of the opposition, ready to break away and defend or attack as they need to. Then there is the

Number Eight, they are steering the ship, screaming commands at the pack. They control the ball as it comes to the back of the pack or add extra weight to the pack if they are not receiving. The Number Eight has the ability to pick and drive with the ball as it is presented to their feet, or act as Scrum half, freeing the Scrum half to provide an extra man to the Backs and create a potential overlap. The Number Eight will also be the first out of the Scrum to attack or defend as necessary.

The complexity of the Scrum is reliant on all players working together. A Scrum that has no unity will breakup and have no effect on the opposition. Each player must work in harmony with the others like bricks in a wall, the power and strength of the Scrum relies on it.

Sometimes we see in life a team trying to accomplish something that seems impossible. History is littered with stories of armies, vastly outnumbered but holding together and working as a team to achieve victory, overcoming great opposition by standing as a combined unit becoming stronger, greater and more powerful.

Sometimes you need propping up when the opposition seems immovable. Sometimes you feel you are head down and working so hard but just need a bit of direction. Sometimes everyone is working so hard but just needs someone to pull you all together to push over the line.

History is littered with teams that have achieved amazing results by working together towards one goal.

Although we are all individuals, we all need each other to work on things that are larger than ourselves. I'm sure we all have had times in our lives when something has seemed daunting, scary or overwhelming but how much less daunting was it when someone said to us, don't worry I will be there with you, to prop you up, help keep you on the straight and narrow, give you a little push to achieve or overcome it. This is how mankind has survived, conquered and achieved throughout history and still does today. This is the sort of support that will get you over the line in any business, personal or sporting situation. We all need a Scrum in our lives because a Scrum becomes more powerful than the sum of its parts... or something like that.

Working within a business and in our personal life we can often feel we are only working to help someone else fulfil their role. We can often feel subordinate rather than equal, but the truth is the result is reliant on all parts of the Scrum working together. It often looks like the main parts are the Hooker or the Number Eight but, if the Locks are not binding together and adding their strength or the Props are not adding support then, the Hooker will not be able to hook the ball. Likewise, the two Locks will not know how the Scrum is performing without the direction of the Number Eight and Flankers.

I am a Lock. I have a deep desire to give my strength and weight to people in my team. I have always given myself to the team and often ploughed ahead with things, thinking it was what was good for the team, not realising that the others in my team were thinking differently. My propensity to power through, and not let anything stop me, often disrupts rather than supports. It is something I often didn`t see as I have a head down attitude. I do, however, have a wonderful Number Eight. She has a great vision and helps steer me when I am off course. She lets me know when to keep going but, even more importantly, when to ease up and play the smart game. I couldn't do what I do without her and I can't thank her enough! Because of this, I find it the easiest thing in the world to be her strength, support and stability when it`s needed. We are a great pack.

"Okay, together we can do this!".

Like the Scrum, the ruck is a brutal thing, but if understood and worked well, it can provide protection against the opposition or take from them what is yours to take. Support is key!

Unlike the Scrum, the ruck can include any player on the pitch. This is not a place for the faint hearted. There used to be a lot of allowances for getting your opponent out of the way if they found themselves on the wrong side of the ruck. This was done by mercilessly raking them out of the way with your studs. There is still an old school mentality that this was when rucking was rucking. Nowadays, if you find yourself on the wrong side of the ruck, you will have to battle hard to free yourself as the opposition can pin you in to get an advantage for you being in an illegal position. Of course, pinning you into the ruck to gain an advantage from your inability to roll away, whilst they protest to the ref that you are obstructing the play is indeed illegal in itself. However, it is often seen by the ref that you need to work harder to get yourself out of that position. The trick is to not be there in the first place, and this is where support is necessary.

The first players into the ruck are the ball carrier and the Tackler. Once a Tackle is made, the ball carrier must release or present the ball back to their side. The Tackler can reach over the ball carrier to retrieve the ball so long as they support themselves on their own legs, once they have released the ball carrier and stood up from the Tackle. This is where support is key. The ball carrier must release the ball back to their side within a short time. They cannot hold on to the ball if the Tackler is taking the ball, in the way just explained, otherwise they will be penalised. Success in the ruck relies on the ball carriers team providing back up. When the Tackler reaches over to take the ball, the ball carriers' team must push them back, forcing them back over the ball and ball carrier to create a shield over the ball. The tackling team can counter push by driving the shielding players back the other way over the ball so that they can again steal the ball. These are brutal hits from one side then the other, driving each other back over the ball to keep or gain possession.

If your teammates do not give you adequate support you can find yourself on the opposition side of the ruck, and in the way of the ball being turned over. This is an illegal position to stay in as you are disrupting play, and if you do not roll out of the way, you will be penalised. You must work hard to wriggle, roll, crawl and scramble out of the ruck on the opposition side. This is vital for your team because you cannot contribute to the play until you have returned to an onside position, behind the back foot of your last teammate in the ruck. You can now re-join the ruck or position yourself in defence. Of course, if you do not roll away, the opposition will be awarded a penalty and, in the right position on the pitch, this can be a better outcome for the opposition than simply turning the ball over as 3 points could be kicked. This means that rolling away might not be as easy as it sounds. An opposition player, say a Prop, joins the ruck and helps drive your team over to gain possession of the ball and you are now underneath him. He puts his knee onto your ribs whilst binding onto his teammates. Not only are you in serious pain but you also are pinned into the ruck when you must roll away. The opposition players start shouting to the ref. that you are obstructing the play and, as long as they are convincing, the ref starts shouting at you, "AWAY! AWAY!". You have no chance. The penalty is awarded.

A good ruck does not need any illegal tactics, however they do happen, often. A good ruck relies on support and hard work. Whether your team is attacking or defending, speedy and definitive support can take possession or protect possession however, both need speedy support.

In all business there is a healthy amount of competition. Whatever industry you are in, you have opposition competing for a limited amount of resources and market share. The market will only be able to sustain a limited amount of competition because there is only a limited amount of market. If things were fair and split equally between everyone, that wanted to be in that particular market, then the shares would be so small that nobody would be able to survive.

Firstly, as mentioned, if you are not well supported, you could find yourself on the wrong side of the ruck. You could get pinned down and be completely helpless, or you are going to get raked out of the way. The word raked here does the act justice, you just have to put 18 stone behind it. It is, and always has been illegal to stamp on a player, however, raking them out of the way with your Rugby studs used to be legal.

Whether you, or your company are trying to get hold of a share of the market in your particular industry, or hold on to the share you have, it is vital that you have support. You are going up against some serious opposition that will not worry about deploying all sorts of tactics, good or bad. If you are not prepared and well supported these tactics can have a devastating effect on your game. Working hard and fast to back each other up is the only way to withstand the onslaught. Likewise, in order to take possession of some much-needed market share, you will have to go fast and hard with a well-rehearsed and planned backup. These times in a young business can be brutally tiring. Constant battling for what seems like the smallest of margins can be soul destroying. It feels like you are just running into a brick wall time after time, but remember, mighty statues are carved out of rock with the smallest of chisels. One thing you can be absolutely certain of is, you will never gain anything if you don't try.

Working as a team means giving strength to those around you. Sometimes you can feel defeated until someone stands by your side, and although they say and do nothing, you stand taller and feel stronger. You get a strength that makes you feel you can keep going. Remember that every time you drive your opposition back, they have to stop you, and that takes energy just like it takes to push them back. Time after time you exhaust them a little more until they break. You have broken through their defence and now you are not making such small margins. You have turned over possession and you are now attacking the Try line for all the glory. Never give up! Organise your attack and support! Keep pounding away at your opposition with every bit of energy you have and when you see your team flagging, stand by them and go again, reminding them that they will break through with persistence and determination!

When I started to write this book, I started to look at the bottom left side of the screen at the word count. It didn't seem to change much from week to week. We were working and it was hard to find time to devote to it. I then started to google "how many words does the average book have". I was almost floored by what was ahead of me. I had been pounding away at the keys for over a year and was still so far away from anything like half of what was needed to be considered a book. I had, at best, produced a pamphlet. I thought it was impossible. What was I doing writing a book, I'm no author? I felt that I had taken on far more than I could deal with and felt like giving up. I tried every page layout and font size to try to make myself feel that I was doing better than I was, like I was making some ground, but it was still the same small number of words compared to what a book should be. I didn't know what to do! I felt demoralised, stupid and out of my depth. I felt I had exhausted everything within me and that there was no way I could produce anything like a book.

I was walking with my girlfriend and our dog one morning around 6am, hand in hand enjoying the cold crisp air and I mentioned that I was finding it difficult to continue writing my book. She said to me that she thought I was doing well and enjoying the process. I explained that it was starting to feel like it was too big a task. It was starting to feel like an absurd idea, and who was I kidding writing a book? I should find something else more constructive to do. She asked me why I wanted to write the book in the first place, knowing full well but wanting me to remember. I stumbled for a while but realised that she was trying to get me to focus on the reason for writing, not the writing itself. Reading and writing are not a skill I have but I wanted to share my philosophy with anyone it might help. She looked at me knowingly and said that although she did not understand Rugby, she did know how to be a team player and would proof-read it for me. I felt air fill my lungs and energy course through my veins, and I had a smile from ear to ear. I felt that with her by my side I could do anything. I felt like this book just got a whole lot better. I had backup and that made me feel like no matter how hard it would be I could count on having her to support to strengthen me.

Brutal, powerful, skilful, but always necessary. This is what Rugby is all about. In most ball sports the aim is to get the ball, that's the target! However, in Rugby the aim is to get the player that has the ball. The Tackle is synonymous with Rugby and once the ball is in the hands of the opposition, its rarely the target. Of course, there are times when a loose pass is intercepted or a ball is kicked and there's a chase for it, but primarily the running game is all about the Tackle in order to stop the advance of the opposition. You must stop the player that has the ball. Once this is done your team can ruck for the ball, but whilst the ball is being played it must be the player with the ball that is targeted.

The perfect Tackle is all about timing. This starts long before any contact with the opposition. First you must track the player that has, or is about to receive, the ball. This means locking onto their movements and positioning yourself in their path, anticipating their running line and preparing yourself for attack. You don't want to sell yourself too early otherwise you are in danger of them changing their line or passing the ball on. Once you have started to move with them, tracking their movements you set yourself low, ready to attack, arms outspread ready to bind onto anything that triggers the trap. The explosive launch of the Tackle in a slightly upwards direction means your shoulder will hit the player around their midriff. Driving all your force in a slightly upwards direction, lifting their weight and taking away their traction from the ground, giving you more traction as your force into the ground has increased. Once your shoulder has connected with the player your arms wrap around the players legs and you squeeze. Squeeze with all your might to stop their legs from running, binding them together so that they can no longer use them for stability, and them with a final drive forwards they fall, crashing down to the ground.

There are many types of Tackle depending on the situation, however, the aim of them all is to stop the advance of the opposition, and timing is everything!!!

If you are chasing down a player that has broken through your defence and making a run for the Try line, or readying yourself to make a head on Tackle, you will need to make sure you time it to perfection. If you don't, there is a real chance you will be left on the floor whilst the opposition gallops away to victory. You usually have one shot as there is no time for recovery.

A well timed and executed Tackle can not only stop the opposition advancing but also change the tempo of the game, your players confidence, the opposition players mindset and, most of all, the atmosphere of the crowd. When the crowd see a big Tackle that drives the player back where they came from, they go crazy. When your team see the Tackle and hear the crowd respond, they get a strength that excites them and drives them on harder and faster. Likewise, when the opposition see their own player not only stopped but dominated and driven back, they all feel the hit. A big dominant Tackle can be felt through the whole team and have a game changing effect.

A dominant Tackle is when a player drives the Tackled player back from the point of the Tackle. This can have a psychological effect as powerful as its physical one. The crowd loves a dominant Tackle, and your team will feel a foot taller and so much stronger as they have shown what they are capable of.

Likewise, a Try-saving Tackle can have a rousing effect on the team. When your opposition has broken through your defence and is making a run for the Try line looking certain to score, you can't give up. You need to give everything to protect your Try line and that means sometimes using every last bit of energy you have. When the opposition is running for a Try and one of your team manages, with every last bit of speed and energy, to chase them down and put in a Tackle that stops them within meters, sometimes millimetres of your Try line, the team and the crowd celebrate like they have scored a Try themselves. After all, you have just avoided losing, potentially, seven points that would require a Try and conversion to counteract, so you could say it is as good as a Try.

In the 2018 Six Nations tournament, England v Wales, the score was 12 – 3 to England and Wales were on the advance.

Around an hour into the game, Anscombe was running the ball back for Wales from their half of the pitch. Wales were offloading the ball well with some quick hands. The ball came to George North who found himself with a two man overlap on his left Wing. Mike Brown of England was in front of him and Scott Williams, North's teammate, to his left. North drew in Brown before passing to Williams. There was nobody in front of Williams and he was inside England's 22m area. Williams sprinted and then dived for the Try on the 5m mark expecting to slide over the line for a Try.

Sam Underhill, who had lost his footing around the halfway line, had recovered and was racing to defend but was a long way back. The Bath Flanker was running with all his might for Williams. Overtaking four Welsh players and four English teammates, he dived for Williams just as Williams dived for the line. Underhill's speed and momentum were so great that he slid, and Just past the 5m mark he connected with Williams, and with just a metre to go he locked an arm around the hip of the Welshman and flipped him onto his back and into touch.

The crowd went wild and Underhill's teammates celebrated with him like he had scored a Try. Williams looked up at Underhill bewildered, wondering where he had come from and how he hadn't scored.

Sam Underhill is a great Tackler and can boast some impressive hits, but this was a Tackle that said, I will never accept defeat. Wales got only three more points on the board and the game finished 12 – 6 to England. If Scott Williams had scored that Try, then Wales could have ended up with another seven points and won the game 12 – 13. Underhill's Tackle was so significant in England's win that everyone was talking about it, and even now I can remember that Tackle, but I can't remember England or Wales scoring the points they took. Underhill's Tackle won the game for England.

The techniques required for different Tackles are many and varied and you could write a book on them, but for the purposes of helping me, I am going to stick to the very basics. Wrap around the middle, slide down to the knees and squeeze.

Tackling has had to undergo a lot of law changes over the years with referees needing to be stricter to protect the Rugby player. The days of the `clothesline` are a thing of the past and a shoulder without an attempt to bind with the arms is a sin binning offence or worse. If you manage to connect with the neck or head with a swinging arm, or a shoulder, then you will see red from the ref. and probably receive a disciplinary ban for a number of matches. The Tackle must be well executed and timed to perfection in order to be effective. Get low and make sure you are in position, so there is no chance of committing a high Tackle even if the player ducks. Make sure you are balanced and can react at the last second to strike. Drive into the hips of your opponent and wrap your arms tightly around them, then slide your arms down around their legs and squeeze them together. Once you have their legs they can't run, they become unbalanced and will fall.

The discipline of the Tackle is all about confidence and control. If you are not confidently going into a Tackle, then you will either be brushed off or get steamrollered, either way you will not be effective. Likewise, making a Tackle can be a brutal and demanding process, there is a real danger of getting hurt if you are not prepared for it. We have all seen players knocked out whilst making a Tackle on an advancing player, for the fundamentally simple reason they had their head on the wrong side of the player as they made the Tackle. It is practice and training that gives a player the discipline and confidence to make an effective Tackle on an advancing player and not get hurt in the process. Putting your head onto the correct side in the Tackle sounds simple and straight forward but it is done in a split second and, when the decision is wrong, then the consequences can be catastrophic. The strongest of players have been left with concussion or worse from a badly executed Tackle. The discipline is all about control.

Control!... Firstly, you must understand what you have control over. You might be able to affect the direction the advancing player is going to take by positioning yourself in a certain place, but this is not control of the player, this is influence over them. They have the choice to pass the ball on, run at you, or try to go around. You have no control over these decisions, you can only influence them. Your teammates might respond to your movements and position, or even your call to cover a position however, this is only influence, as they might not understand or hear your call, they might not see your movements and not respond to them. Therefore, you can only have influence over them, not control. You might anticipate the play the opposition is trying to make, and organise your team to counteract the attack, however, they might change the play. You therefore don't have control, just influence over the play.

The only control you have is over you and this means you must be prepared and confident, otherwise the influence the other players on the pitch have over you can put you in a position you didn't anticipate. When positioning yourself to make the Tackle you have to be in control of yourself. If you let yourself be influenced by the attacking player, they will put you in a position you do not want to be. They might do this with a dummy pass or a step or jink, to make you think they are going one way, then step and go the other. It's important that you keep control, position yourself, and when the time is right, spring the trap with confidence, power, and, above all, control. Put your head on the correct side of the Tackle and bind on using the power of that shoulder to drive through the player dominating them in the Tackle.

As there are so many variations on the Tackle, and quite frankly, no set Tackle! It is just the process of stopping the advance of the attacking player. There are of course, many rules regarding tackling which are important to know because you might be handing victory to the opposition if you don't keep to the rules. When the game comes down to the wire it is often not the Try that wins the game but relentless defending. Tackle after Tackle, defending phase after phase of attack with complete control to not give away a penalty.

France v New Zealand in the Quarter Final of the 2007 World Cup. After the memorable Haka faceoff between the two teams, with the French lined up right on the halfway line dressed in The Tricolour colours, with the All Blacks edging closer to the halfway line, until both teams are within touching distance of each other. France knew they were up against the best attacking team in the world and would have to play a very defensive game if they were to survive. Dave Ellis was the defensive Coach for the French team and when interviewed he said the French knew they could beat the All Blacks, but they had to defend in different ways. They started with the traditional defensive plan of targeting the legs, but in the second half, when they knew the All Blacks had stamina and strength, they started to use a 2-man Tackle strategy, now adopted by most teams and known as the Choke Tackle. This meant that New Zealand had to commit more players to the contact area reducing their attacking options. France made 299 Tackles with half of the French team making over 25 Tackles each. Beating the All Blacks in a Rugby World Cup Quarter Final was the result of a very well-planned defensive strategy.

Another example of the Tackle winning a game was in the 2015 Six Nations competition between Wales and Ireland. The score was 15 – 9 to Wales early in the second half of the game and Ireland had a Lineout inside the Welsh half. Ireland needed a Try and conversion to go ahead and they were on the attack. The Lineout went to plan, and they started to attack Wales. Wave after wave of attack and Wales kept putting in the Tackles. Ireland tried moving the ball out wide, they tried running at Wales, they even tried creating a maul, but they couldn't get through the Welsh defence. They pushed on to Wales 5m line but couldn't find a way through. Wales were controlled and disciplined in their defence, not giving away a penalty. Wales withstood thirty two consecutive phases of attack until Ireland gave away a penalty for not releasing. Moments later Ireland had another lineout, this time inside the Welsh 22m. Again, Ireland went on the attack, firstly with a driving maul from the Lineout and then breaking off to run in the Try. Wales were again, controlled and disciplined. Ireland were within 1m of the Try line and, at one point, over the Try line but Wales held them up and drove them back. Another thirteen consecutive phases of attack and again Ireland gave away a penalty. Wales had survived again, and won because of discipline, confidence, and above all, control, not giving away a penalty.

When I find myself under pressure, whether at work or in my private life, I always find that things turn out fine if I stay calm and controlled. It seems, on the flipside, that things go from bad to worse when I panic or let the situation affect me. I find that I make the wrong decisions because I have let something, or someone, influence me to do or act differently to the way I felt I should. Often negativity can influence you to be negative and this means you lose control of the positive decisions you would usually make. Realising that being influenced in a negative way opens myself up to being steamrolled or even worse knocked out, metaphorically, I started to be more positive and be in control of the way I was influenced.

I have never been one to enjoy confrontation, however, in a previous role as a Contract's Manager for a Construction Company I regularly found myself right in the middle of it. And when I say the middle of it, I mean it was coming at me from all sides. Clients were unhappy with anything from cost to progress and wanted to know what was going to be done about it. Contractors were unhappy with the price for their part of the contract and didn't want to continue without more money. The boss wanted to save money and to get the work completed faster and the employees wanted a pay rise and to knock off at 4pm. I found myself becoming stressed. I knew that every day I went to work, I would have to have a confrontation with someone with varying degrees of stress. I remember getting an email from a client who was a rather difficult man. He was unreasonable, rude, and according to him, always right. He wanted to see me because he was fed up with the way the project was progressing. I knew he was wanting to vent some anger, for whatever reason, and looking for confrontation. I decided I was not going to be influenced by him, and that meant taking control of myself. Hating the idea of confrontation, I knew I had to be in control of my emotions in order to stop the attack. I had to dominate the Tackle, I needed to steady myself, focus on the job and drive him back before he made any gains, but not with negative confrontation, he had this in spades and was ready to use it, I had to be positive, confident and in control. I arrived at the house and didn't give myself time to be influenced by him. I walked in and before he had a chance to be confrontational, with the biggest smile I could make, I stuck out my hand and told him how nice it was to see him. I went on to say how great the place was looking and pointed out a few features that I knew he was particularly pleased about. He was so surprised by my enthusiasm and positivity he couldn't help but agree. I then said that I knew he had said in his email he was unhappy, and I was here to make it right for him. I understood he was frustrated with the way he felt things were progressing and I insisted I was going to make sure every effort was made to rectify things. He suddenly started backtracking and apologising for being abrupt in his email. It turned out he was feeling unhappy to come home every day to a building site. We agreed that we would work on areas to make it more homely for him and he was so thankful. He apologised for the way he had been, and I was on my way having diverted an attack and left feeling like I had won the cup, let alone the match.

When you are a business that has some aggressive competition, it is often difficult not to be influenced by them. They might have what you want, whether it is a particular client, technology, or market share and you can find yourself reacting to their influence over you. Or it might be you that has something they want, either way, you must be in control of yourself. Keeping an eye on the play, you must set yourself in the position you need to be in. You are only in control of yourself so be prepared for what you need to do and, above all be disciplined, you do not want to give away possession for the sakes of not being disciplined it could cost you the game. Always remember, if you are confident, positive and controlled you will have an impact, a powerful, game changing impact!

In true Rugby Union style the process of throwing the ball
back onto the pitch is just the most complicated affair. The
Lineout is like no other sport. The rules that surround the
Lineout seem so complicated, but to see it in action and
performing at its best is a magnificent thing.

Two lines of players, a metre apart, looking to catch the ball
as it is thrown down the middle of them. The team putting in
the throw has a secret code, a call to let the team know
where the ball is to be thrown. This used to be a very scrappy
display with both teams jumping into the path of the ball,
hoping to bat the ball back to their own side and even with a
secret call, it was anyone`s for the taking. To make it more
difficult for the opposition they would throw the ball high so
that the players had to jump to get the ball. The jumping
players were usually the Locks, among the tallest on the
pitch, giving them the advantage, however, this gave the
opposition a clue as to the target of the ball so they would
line up the Locks with the Locks or taller players with the
taller players, levelling the playing field so to speak.

As the throws got more accurate, they also gained more
height so that the jumping players were not only trying to
outwit their opponents but also out jump them, the
difference being fingertip stuff. I am unsure when players

started to be lifted in the line out, but I remember when the rule was that a player could be `supported` once they had jumped, but not `lifted`, in the line out, no pre-grip from the supporting player on the jumping player. This became a bit of a joke considering the height players were getting as they were jumping. Generally, the two players either side of the jumper would, with straight arms, catch the jumping player as they jumped and, moving towards each other, their straight arms would push the jumper up into the path of the ball. This was not lifting, just supporting, as lifting was illegal. However, in 1999 lifting in the line-out was finally legalised under Law 18.

Whether you are an old school purist or a lover of the technical progression of the game you cannot help but be amazed at the height these players get when jumping/being lifted in the line out. These players are catching a ball that is around 13ft or 4m off the ground, and considering the average man is 5ft 9in or 1.75m, this is an impressive feat. This is the result of pushing the boundaries, challenging and being challenged. Competition will always lead to bigger and better things. I just can't imagine how high they will be jumping in another 10 years` time, but in training they push the boundaries further and further to get that fingertip advantage. After all, it is the small margins that make the difference between winning and losing.

When it comes to support these players need all they can get. To say this is a team effort is obvious as the chance of challenging for the ball without the support from the lifters is as close to impossible as it gets. To receive a ball that is being passed over your head by double your own height requires help. Not only do you need to get there but you need to get there at the right time and be stable enough to catch the ball and distribute it as the play predicts.

The support act is usually provided by the strong stable Props. The Hooker usually makes the throw, calling the play for timing sakes. In modern games there is a lot of changing places going on to confuse the opposition but when the position is set, the Hooker throws with accuracy, speed and power. The jumping player rises from the ground, lifted into the path of the ball by their strong and powerful teammates, holding them there as the ball, spinning beautifully, drills straight into their huge waiting hands. They either pass the ball back to the Scrum half (off the top ball) or keep possession of it until they land (driven ball).

Once the play has been made, the jumping players must be brought down from on high safely. This is not a position you want to be left in to make your own way down, especially as the commotion below will suddenly become a maul. Being brought down safely is as important as being lifted in the first place. This is most apparent after seeing players abandoned at full stretch by their lifting teammates resulting in a fall onto the players below. Their legs get tangled and knocked on the players below them and they come crashing down on their heads, often resulting in serious injury.

The trust between these players is gained on the training ground, lift after lift after lift. Once the player is lifted, they have a lot to do, especially if they are contesting for the ball, they will need stability if they are going to be successful. This trust gives them the confidence to stretch further and reach higher, always knowing they are in safe hands. The support they have is refined with practice and discipline. The discipline needed by all players to be successful in the Lineout is more about timing than power and strength. Yes, these two are important, but timing is key.

The discipline to listen to the call and be patient in the moment is the most important part of the lineout. It might look like no time has been taken but the movement of getting into position is the big giveaway to the opposition. Even with all the changing of places in the lineout, when the jump is about to take place, it's obvious to all. The jumper crouches and the two Forwards either side of them bind onto their muscular legs. As they jump, they crouch and stand up under them, lifting them as high as they can into the path of the ball. This process takes time to set, and the opposition, if well-drilled, can follow the movements and see when their counterparts are ready to lift. This means that if the timing is too early you might be up in the air waiting for the ball and suddenly be joined by your opposite number just a few inches in front of you, with their mighty hands outspread to intercept the ball before it gets to you. Likewise, if you spend too much time getting ready to lift, you might end up seeing the ball sail over your heads, bouncing loose in field for anyone to claim. As with all patience, time can seem like it stands still, however, even though we are talking split second stuff, patience in the moment is what wins you the ball.

The call, or decision of play, is made by the leader of the lineout, the Lineout Captain or whatever the title is for them. The Lineout team huddle together before approaching the Lineout and the decision is made by the Lineout captain for their setup. As they approach, the Lineout captain usually is the last to arrive, studying the opposition to see how they are lining up. Are there any obvious weaknesses in their line up? Are there any mismatches between opposite numbers? Are either side consistent in their ability to compete in the air or on the ground when the ball is brought down to drive through? All these things are going through the mind of the Lineout Captain and when they know what they want to do… they call. This call is loud, clear and short, but coded. They want all their team to understand the plan with absolute clarity, but for all others to be confused.

There is so much secrecy in life that codes are used all the time, from the Secret Services and Police, to the parents trying to decide whether to get their kids an ice cream and once the code is broken you are at the mercy of the opposition. If the kids think there is a chance of ice cream, you might as well give up. At home we never use the word "walk", unless we intend taking our wonderful little dog for a walk. She is always listening out for it, and if mentioned in passing, then you might as well get the lead and put your boots on because she won't leave you alone until she gets one. We use all sorts of code words instead, however, never underestimate your opponent. Our little dog listens so intently that she starts to understand the code. Words we rely on such as `trundle`, `wander` and `stroll`, start to be recognised by her as being associated around the time she is due a walk. Her head cocks to one side and she gives you a look as if to say, "yes… go on… what were you about to say???".

The code is therefore something that needs to be constantly changed so as to keep your plans between you and your team. If the opposition are listening and observing, then they will start to understand the code and be able to anticipate your jump. Likewise, the code must be understood by all in your team. If there is a misunderstanding, then you will lose the lineout. The call is discussed in training and practiced over and over so that it is understood by all and becomes as clear as the Queens English.

And so, with a loud and clear voice, the Lineout call is made. The Hooker knows exactly where to throw the ball. Their teammates know exactly who is jumping and who is supporting. All the team know if the ball will be off the top or brought down for a maul, and with precision, accuracy and timing the plan is executed. The ball is drilled straight into the hands of the jumping player and the Lineout is won.

There is so much competition these days in business and life in general. From rival company's trying to get one step ahead of you, to the Jones's, and we know how hard it is competing with them. If you are going to compete then you have to make sure your team understands the plan. Never hide the plan from your team. You all have an eye on the ball, so it is imperative you all understand the plan to get it.

Although, in Rugby, the process of throwing the ball back onto the pitch is so complicated, when everyone is working as a team, it is also impressive. Life is never straight forward, especially when you are trying to achieve great heights, but with teamwork making the difference it can also be extraordinary. To reach great heights takes collaboration, cooperation, teamwork and effort from all.

You will reach far higher and achieve
far more when you give your
strength to others!

The most successful business individuals in the world such as Bill Gates, Richard Branson, Warren Buffett, and so many more, do not take sole acknowledgment for their achievements. They are always the first to praise, reward and respect the guys, the team, that helped them get there, because everyone benefits. Achievement starts with assembling a team, bringing everyone together for the same goal. Only when everyone in your team is working together in the realisation that if one achieves, all achieve, then you will all succeed. The aim of success is to succeed! It sounds obvious but so often this simple principle is misunderstood. Success means everyone playing their part to win one ball. If one player feels that they are more important then the ball will be lost, you can't compete against a good team thinking you are the most important in yours, you have to value each individual position equally and realise that without them all there is no success. The overriding principle in this book is `teamwork`! Whether you are a one-man band, family member, single or part of a large company, teamwork is where you can succeed!

` Success` means different things to different people. Everyone has different values in life and for different reasons, this usually is moulded by individual and past experiences. When we have enjoyed certain things or times, we want to have that feeling of enjoyment again, that is to be human. We are emotional beings and that means we react differently to things based on how we have felt in the past. If we have a bad experience with one thing or another then we get the same feeling when we have to do that thing again. It's an inbuilt safety mechanism in us to protect us from danger or harm. Likewise, when we have had a good experience, we naturally want to replicate the feeling and that makes us look forward to doing that thing again.

Because we have had so many different experiences, we all have so many different likes and dislikes, mostly irrational but, always emotional. This means our wants are so very different and therefore `success` becomes a very individual thing. One person might see success as achieving in business or society. A Rugby player might say success is being the best in their position. Another person could say success is making a difference to others. Whatever your individual understanding of success is it is always based on your values, however, being successful will never be achieved on your own. I challenge anyone to give me a case where someone has achieved without any influence, help or interaction from another human being. The motive for success can be selfish but the achievement of it is never without a team of some sort or another.

The Great Sir Isaac Newton, a leading mind of his day and considered one of the greatest minds of all time, said, "If I have seen a little further, it is by standing on the shoulders of giants."

I'm not sure Isaac Newton played Rugby in the late 1600's but he certainly understood the principles of the line out. He recognised that he could not have achieved the great heights he did without the support of other great men and women.

Not all of us were blessed with good looks. Some of us were blessed with Brawn, and a few got brains.

The division in the Rugby team of the Backs and Forwards is a strange phenomenon. The jobs these two groups of players have to do is quite different and therefore filled by quite different players.

The Backs are graceful, fast and beautifully formed and are pivotal in getting the ball over the line. The Forwards are big strong and terrifying in appearance. More often than not it is expected that the ball is won and protected by the Forwards and passed to the Backs to make gains and score the Try.

I'm sure that by now you are ahead of me... it is not difficult to see where this is going. Two very different groups. They train differently, they work differently, they have different jobs, and, because of the different jobs, they tend to have different skills, different physiques, however, one without the other will not win the game. Imagine a team made up entirely of Lock Forwards. It might be a scary thought, but they are never going to win a game. I reckon a good Lock Forward has about 20 yards at full pace in them at best and then they are spent, so those on the Wings are going to be wasted long before they reach the Try line. Likewise, the

Backs would struggle to put in a good Scrum. There are the exceptions to the rule, but they are few and far between.

Once a young player starts to favour the Backs or the Forwards, they start to develop different attributes. Their bodies start to respond to the different stresses and strains they are under. They start to become heavier and stronger if they are a Forward and often this has an impact on their speed. The Backs start to become faster and more nimble and therefore become more streamlined for want of a better word.

These two different groups, however, make up the Rugby team. Very different players playing the same game on the same team, working in perfect harmony towards the same goal... or that is the idea at least.

When working together in a team it is vitally important that everyone knows the skills and abilities of their teammates, the roles they have to play and how you are going to interact and work together. Very early on in our company there were two of us and many roles to fill. I would try to do things if I thought they needed doing because we were so busy. I felt as though I was helping to keep the cogs turning by carrying out all the jobs that needed doing when I had the time. In my head I was just getting things done! However, this is not how it was seen by my partner. It often resulted in me completing jobs that were not my responsibility, and not very efficiently, and not dealing with tasks that I was responsible for. This wasn't working smart! I was hindering her position and not doing mine. In reality, I was out of position and not ready to receive the ball and therefore it was dropped. She has a very good understanding of the importance of doing your job. This isn't to say you can't lend a hand or support, but you must be in position when the ball is passed your way.

My son would get frustrated on the Wing if the ball wasn't getting out wide. He wanted, so much, to get involved in the game that he had a tendency, probably inherited from me, to start creeping into other positions. Not satisfied with being out on the Wing, with little involvement, he would drift in field in search of some action. Thinking this would be helpful he would end up going for the same ball as the Centre and end up tripping over each other or knocking on because the Centre, thinking this was his ball, was suddenly joined by an out of position Winger. Inevitably, when the ball did finally get out wide there was no Winger to receive it and he was rightly rebuked for being out of position. Maybe I'm being a little hard on him to make a point as he was very young at the time, however, when he started to play more competitively in the older age groups, he started to understand the importance of sticking to your position and letting everyone else play theirs.

We can't all play the same position, so why are we trying to be like everyone else.

You are different to the rest of your team, but that means you fit in, so embrace it.

Find your position and be the best `You` you can be!

I remember one game, when my son was an under 15, he came in at half time so frustrated that the ball was not getting to him. Possession was being kicked away, or the Centres were running sideways, leaving him no space, or trying to break through when he had space on the overlap. He was fuming at half time, protesting to his teammates that there was "so much space on the Wing, just get the ball out there". The second half started the same as the first half had ended and I could see him trying to focus on sticking to his position. They were three points down to the opposition with about ten minutes to go. His team were on the attack and he had space on the right Wing. The ball went through the hands of the Centres and the outside Centre started drifting across the pitch towards him. The opposition, realising they were leaving an opening started to close him down, he screamed for the ball and the Centre passed him a great ball into his path. With the momentum he had, and the space in front of him he turned on the speed and the opposition couldn't get close. He ran the ball over the line and under the posts. They converted with ease and won the game by four points. He wasn't frustrated after the game, he was delighted.

Once I understood that trying to micromanage our business was the same as trying to play every position on the pitch, I started to give the team some space. Of course, I was watching, overseeing, communicating, influencing and supporting, but doing MY job. Things started to get done so much easier and quicker. The quality also improved as there weren't two people trying to do the same thing and getting in each other's way. Even when I think I have some time; I support rather than interfere. I'm there if anyone needs me and I will let them know by communicating that, but I won't go looking to get involved until I'm called upon. It might just take up too much of my time, leaving me not able to fulfil my position.

The team is made up of very different people with very different skills. It's important that you all understand each other's abilities so that they can be used effectively. Building a good team is important and you need to employ people with the skills to do the job you need doing, otherwise you are going to be playing two positions, and that is never going to benefit the team.

When building a team, you must first analyse the positions. A team plays a certain way and that will always determine the type of player it needs. Of course, there is a need to work with the team you have, however, there is always a certain game plan that is implemented. In any sport, when there is a change of Manager, Head Coach or Owner, there is always a shift in the way the team is expected to play. This is the game plan. Sometimes clubs employ a Head Coach because they have turned around previous teams and they think theirs would benefit, or sometimes they are just in need of a change at the top because things have become lack lustre.

Whatever the reason, there is always a change in tempo, a change in mood and mentality. There is always a change in the way they are going to play. There is a new game plan. This plan sets the need to have the right player for the position. Players get drafted in and players get drafted out. The team changes because the new management is trying to change the way they want the team to perform.

Some teams have an established Manager that is set in their ways, and they look for players they can use or develop to perform as the position dictates. Other teams change their Manager, and the players either change and adapt to the new position and perform as the new management expects, or they are replaced by a player that will.

We have all come to expect this type of management change in sports, but we don't seem to be as comfortable with it in business. Supporters cry out for change when a team is constantly performing badly, crying out for the Manager to go. In a lot of cases over the years even the Chairman or Owner are the target of the supporters' desire for change at the top. However, when a business is seemingly `going down`, there is always an air of anger when new management is implemented and they start replacing, getting rid of, or drafting in new members of a team to get it back to winning ways. We have all heard the stories of new management just getting rid of people, replacing them with others, seemingly just changing things up for the sakes of it.

I'm not condoning management changes that come in gung-ho, thinking that changing staff will solve everything, getting rid of the underperforming and replacing them. No! the principle of a change of management is that the game plan changes, not necessarily the players. Many players go from club to club, underperforming at some and outperforming at others. Those that are outperforming get pursued by bigger and better clubs, however, when they make the change to the bigger, better club they underperform. This isn't because they don't try as hard, they just aren't suited to the way the team plays the game, the game plan. When a new Manager takes over a team some players perform better, and some don't. This is because the game plan is different, and they are being asked to perform differently.

When a company's management is changed because the Company is underperforming it is vital the game plan changes, and for the better. This means that everyone in the team must adjust to the new way of play. Some will outperform and others will underperform. If the underperformers cannot adapt and develop to be outperformers, then they will not be a help to the team. Sadly, this is not good for the team or the direction of the Company. They must be replaced with others that can strengthen the team so they can all outperform and subsequently succeed. Many new Managers draft in players that do not seem to have had much success at other clubs but the Manager knows they play the kind of Rugby they need to build the team. Supporters question why the new Manager has drafted in this player after they underperformed at their last club but the Manager has a game plan and this player has all the right skills to play that role within that new game plan.

This is the way of things, and although we don't like the thought of people being fired or replaced it is often, but not always, the case that it works out for them. They find somewhere that better suits them where they can perform more effectively and find more enjoyment or passion in their work. After all, if the change in game plan is not made and the team continues to underperform then the team faces certain relegation, at best to a league they can perform in, with a drop in financial benefit or, ultimately, certain and final closure. Nobody wants to see the closure of a club.

Chris Ashton has had a career that has been a bit up and down, like his trademark `swan dive`. However, after returning to England, to Sale Sharks in July 2018 from French side Toulon, and scoring against England for the Barbarians, he had a short spell back in the national side. He seemed to be enjoying his Rugby and Sale seemed to be enjoying success, but in March 2020 it was announced that his contract at Sale was terminated with immediate effect. When the Director of Rugby, Steve Diamond, was asked, he said that it was simply down to a disagreement over how the Rugby at Sale would be played. "There is no situation" he said, "just a disagreement on how we want to play the game". The Manager had a clear game plan and Ashton didn't want to play that way. Even though Ashton was still playing some very good Rugby he didn't want to adapt and develop the way Sale wanted him to. A day later it seemed that Harlequins thought that, although he didn't fit the position at Sale, he would be a good fit for them and announced they had signed Ashton with immediate effect.

It is vital you build your team with a clear game plan in mind. Find the right player for the role that is determined by the game plan, not just by the players attributes. If you pick your team on the merit of the player only, you will have lots of really talented individuals that have no ability to work with each other. Your game plan dictates the qualities of the position and your ability to get the best player to fulfil that position is key to the success of the team.

The Rugby team is made up of some very different shapes and sizes, however, they all combine to become greater than the sum of their parts. The success of a team is reliant on all parts working together for one goal... The Try.

A team works together like a well-oiled and calibrated machine, working in harmony towards one goal. So does a car engine. However, a `great` team has one more thing far more important to a team's success and that is team spirit!

Collins dictionary says, "Team spirit is the feeling of pride and loyalty that exists among the members of a team that makes them want their team to do well or to be the best."

When a team is working together with pride it means they are pleased with the achievements that are being made and will work harder to achieve more for their team.

Likewise, when a team has loyalty, a strong feeling of support and allegiance its players feel the necessity to give themselves for the good of their teammates, not themselves. This means they do not consider themselves first when they are playing, they try to achieve for their team first. This mentality means they work harder for the many, rather than for themselves. When you set goals to achieve for yourself you tend to be very lenient, however, if you are trying to achieve for someone else you will work far harder for them because the pride you feel for them is far greater than from yourself.

Loyalty can be scarce in everyday life, however, in a Rugby team it is second nature. Working hard for each other comes naturally to the Rugby player because they can't win on their own. Without a team there is no Try, so a Rugby player has a need to have loyalty and protect the loyalty their teammates feel for them.

Once team spirit is created in a team it elevates them to a different class. They don't just work well together; they want to work well together to succeed. They don't just want to perform well; they want to perform well for their teammates and want their teammates to perform well also.

This desire to achieve and perform for the team gives the individuals extra purpose and determination to succeed. It is like an electricity that surges through a team energizing them to become greater. They want to please their teammates and, in turn, get so much more pleasure from the win because they see the elation on their teammates faces and know they helped put it there.

At home we say we are a team. That means we are all working for each other. If one of us is achieving, we are all achieving. If one of us is struggling, we all give our support to help them over the line. We never have the feeling of having the world on our shoulders because there is always a teammate to help us out, even if that is just to listen. It means someone is giving their time for me so that I am not struggling on my own. Also, it is a word we use if one of us seems inconsiderate or selfish over a matter, we just utter the word, "team!" and that makes them realise we are feeling they are not being a team player. Our desire to help and perform for our teammates gives us a motivation to perform to our best and more. "For the team!"

We follow a great Captain into battle because they inspire us
with confidence and strength. All great teams have a great
Captain or leader, the motivation, the heart and soul. They
have an ability to make you feel invincible when you
previously felt vulnerable. The Captain doesn't always need
to say anything, just standing tall radiating a strength that
flows through all those that stand by them. Causing that
intensity to well up in their followers that replicates their
own, creating an army of themselves multiplied by its
numbers.

2003 World Cup winner Neil Back was interviewed and
mentioned that Martin Johnson, the England, British and Irish
Lions and Leicester Tigers Captain would always stop in the
tunnel leading the team onto the pitch. He would turn to
them and give them a few rousing words to get them all
focused and stirred up for the game. However, Back said he
would never forget Johnson leading them out for the World
Cup Final against Australia onto the Telstra Stadium pitch.
The biggest game of all their careers, not only against
England's biggest adversary, but playing away in their
country. This was the climax of four years of hard work,
training, planning, relentless focus and determination. This
was the game they started to train for after being knocked
out of the world cup in 1999. This was it, and they were

being led out by an awe-inspiring Captain that had experience, strength, power and leadership.

Back said that Johnson stopped in the tunnel, as he always did, he turned to face his team and looked at them for a moment. Then, without saying a word, turned and walked out onto the pitch. Back said they had all expected the same positive message, rally cry or rousing speech, but there were no words, just a look. Back said in that moment they were all gelled as a team, behind a great Captain, they then followed that Captain out onto the battlefield.

A few weeks later he asked Johnson why he hadn't said anything when he was leading them out onto the pitch. Johnson explained that when he turned, he looked into the eyes of all the players and he knew they were ready, he didn't have to say anything.

A Captain like Martin Johnson has the ability to give his strength to anyone who follows him. Everyone in his team played with the same passion and determination as Martin Johnson that day. If asked, I suspect every one of those players would say the outcome would have been very different if there had been a different Captain leading them out. However, if Martin Johnson was asked who made the difference on the day, I suspect he would say every player on the pitch came together as one team.

Sarah Hunter won the Rugby World Cup in 2014 with England and went on to become England Captain. In 2016 she was awarded World's Best Player and told the BBC in an interview, "It's fantastic to get the award and recognition, but it doesn't really sit very comfortably with me. Rugby is the ultimate team sport and to be singled out for an award just seems not quite right. I wouldn't be where I am or be able to perform the way I did to get this award without my teammates around me."

A Captain's ability to bring a team together is never more recognised than when a team is in trouble. No matter how good a team is, the Captain is the decision maker and, as a result can change the outcome of the game positively and negatively, rarely does a good team have a bad Captain. If a good team has been assembled it has usually been built around a good Captain, and this Captain has often been in the team for a while. They know the players individually and the team as a whole. They understand the motivations they have and need. This gives them the ability to make the right choices during the game and motivate their team to react and adapt where necessary.

Sometimes a team can be limited. For instance, some nations have produced a few very good players but are unable to produce enough for a team to compete at the highest level. One team that springs to mind is Italy. They have always been the underdogs when playing on the big stage, but they had a Captain that led by example. Sergio Parisse is considered one of the best Number Eights to have played the game, however, he was on a side that was limited by numbers. Parisse, however, has shown on many occasions that leading from the front can raise a team to another level. We talked about Team Spirit and how this can elevate a team to compete with teams that would normally be out of their league. Every team that came up against Parisse`s Italy, gave them the same respect they would give the best in the world. Every team understands the value a great Captain and player like Parisse gives their team. They either respect it or fall foul of an upset by the underdogs.

Fans of Rugby might say that teams like Italy are no threat, but when they are beaten by them they very quickly realise that a Team's Spirit can be a mighty force. Take Japan in the 2015 World Cup who beat South Africa 34-32. Then in the 2019 RWC reaching the quarter finals after beating Russia, Ireland, Samoa and Scotland on the way, sadly to be undone by none other than South Africa. The Japanese team has cemented themselves in World Rugby as giant killers. They will never play another team who will not have respect for their tenacity, determination and team spirit for a very long time.

The Captain is the decision maker and can influence a team negatively as well as positively. If you are in a position of command, whatever that might be, there is always a danger of feeling like you have got everything under control when things are going well. This false sense of security can be your, and your teams, downfall. As all good Captains know, there will always be another storm.

"In calm water, every ship has a good Captain." Grover Cleveland.

The Captain's ability to be prepared for every eventuality is key to their success. They are always studying the next game. They are always focused on what is in front of them, to the side of them and behind them, as well as having one eye on what is ahead. When they are not playing, they are studying their opponents. A Captain never has the luxury of rest because they are the ones who rally the team in the moment.

As the phrase goes, "if you fail to prepare, prepare to fail". A Captain that is not prepared is heading for disaster. When things are going well a Captain can think they are doing well, but this is often not the case. Many teams have been enjoying a large lead at half time only to be beaten in the second half because they thought they had it all under control. It is the Captain's responsibility to focus their team and not let complacency creep in.

In the 1999 Rugby World Cup semi-final France faced New Zealand at Twickenham. New Zealand were favourites to win the game and France hadn't been given a hope against a New

Zealand side with the awesome Jonah Lomu. Although France scored first, they went in at half time trailing 17-10.

French Captain Raphael Ibanez recalled his side still being hopeful. He told his team "I totally believe we can do it! We are close to doing something great. It is somehow within our grasp."

Shortly after the restart the mighty Lomu struck again making the score 24-10. Despite the score the French still felt they could do something. Together, they all felt they were capable of pulling off something great against such a formidable team.

Christophe Lamaison slotted home two drop goals and the momentum started to swing Frances way. Then, after two converted penalties by France the difference was reduced to two points. Josh Kronfeld, New Zealand's No.7, said "it's called panic". He said, "you're in a comfortable situation then everything changes". He said for 40 minutes they were playing catch up. "You start thinking, oh my goodness they're getting closer, oh my goodness we have to score. And then it's gone." The French ran in a Try to take the lead and never stopped. They beat New Zealand 43-31 in one of the greatest comebacks in Rugby. New Zealand Captain Taine Randell did not have an answer to the French change of game plan, belief and team spirit.

When you have responsibility for a team, as a leader, you must be the one that can unite them. The team's strength is in its unity and that unity is cemented by the Captain. If you have the following of a team and you believe, they believe, but if you crumble, they crumble too. You are one team and therefore you stand and fall as one.

When a team wins the competition it's the Captain that gets to lift the trophy. This is because they are the one that has to be accountable for the team when they have had a bad game. The Captain is the one who has to account for the way the team performed to the fans and the media. The Captain is the one who answers for the individual players and stands up for them when everyone is criticising them. The Captain is the one who takes the criticism and protects the team. And it's the Captain that lifts the team when they are down. When there are questions to be answered the Captain is the one to answer them. Brian O'Driscoll said, "When you are Captain, you are never speaking for yourself."

As a Captain, you protect your team, you put them and their needs first. You lead by example and take all the persecution for them. You give your all to them and never expect them to do anything you wouldn't do. You're working when your team is resting. When the game is tough and your team is on its knees you are the one that stands up and carries your team to the end.

That's why the team stands behind the Captain when the Captain lifts the trophy... for them!

My kids say jokingly of their schoolteachers, "if you can't do, teach!". That said, it's interesting how many School Teachers become very accomplished professional Sports Coaches, including the former Ireland Head Coach, Joe Schmidt, Stuart Lancaster, Ex Head Coach of England, current Head Coach of England, Eddie Jones, Dave Rennie the Head Coach of Australia and many more. Rennie said of his former and current jobs, "Teaching, Coaching, it's the same thing, the kids are just a bit bigger."

The game of Rugby has developed over the years, becoming professional and evolving as the players become more technical. The position of Head Coach, Manager, Director of Rugby, Gaffer, Boss, or whatever the title, has become a far more technical and involved job that carries so much responsibility. The Coach spends so much of their time focusing on developing the finest details and minute margins of their team that it is more than a full-time job. The Coach therefore employs staff that specialise in the different elements of the game to make the smallest improvements to gain the smallest margins on the field. It is the smallest margins that can win a game, and it doesn't matter if you win by one point, what matters is you win!

The modern Coach is obsessed with the smallest margins. Anyone that plays sport competitively will try to improve daily even when they are the best in their sport. In 2016 Sarah Hunter was the world's best player, however, she went to training the day after she was awarded the accolade and, with the same determination and dedication, she tried to improve her game. Why? Because when you are the best everyone is trying to be better than you, and if you don't improve you will be very quickly overtaken and left behind. This mind set is in every team Coach.

Arguably the best club side in history is the Canterbury Crusaders, not only due to having some of the greatest players of all time in the squad over the years, they have also had record breaking players making for a record breaking club. As the worlds` most successful Rugby club they have achieved ten title wins, been finalists fifteen times and semi-finalists nineteen times in twenty four years of Super Rugby. They are also the only Super Rugby team to complete a whole season undefeated.

As a club they have a winning Coach with a winning mentality. Scott (Razor) Robertson was overlooked for the ultimate job in Rugby, to be Coach of The All Blacks. He seemed the right choice considering he had led the Crusaders from the 2017 season, on a run of fifty three games, in which they won forty eight of them, only losing five times. He was interviewed about missing out on the opportunity and he replied, "I have a little bit of a plan of how I can get better, that's one thing I've got to do as a Coach, so the next time it comes around I'm even better than I am now."

This mentality of constant improvement is key to any Coach's success. They start with themselves, and then the team, but it never stops there. They have an ingrained desire to improve and be the best in everything they do. This desire means the team feels the necessity to improve without being told. The desire becomes infectious as every player knows, if you want to become the best you have to improve, and if you want to stay the best you have to continue to improve. This is the fundamental principle a Coach instils in their team.

Every good Coach understands what they have and is mindful of the individuals of the team. Their strengths and weaknesses, skills both physical and mental and their abilities to strengthen and bind a team. The Coach must know what they have to improve before they can improve it.

The building of a team is reliant on understanding how the individuals will work together within the team. Building, balancing, and improving takes years of knowledge on how individuals work together. The Coach must be a Master of Psychology in order to get the best from the team. Not only will they need to consider the individual players wants and desires to play in a certain position, or with certain other players, but they also need to consider the team as a whole.

Building, balancing and improving a team is not for the faint hearted.

When things are going well you feel invincible but when things are not working it's the Coach's head on the block. I'm sure we have all felt the pressure when we have had responsibility for something and we would do anything to improve the situation, including doing it all yourself, but that is very rarely a solution. Seeing Coaches in the box at a Rugby game, banging, smashing, upturning and throwing anything in their path as their team is losing. Once they have composed themselves to do the post-match interview, they begin with the positives. "We were dominant in a certain half or area, we worked hard here or there" … and then they start with the improvement. "We need to look at our play in this or that and improve here or there…" and so on. This is all a polite way of saying they were not good enough. This composure and polite dialogue rarely lasts until they enter the team changing room where, true to someone with their head on the block, they tell the team what they really thought. This is a defence of their ability to Coach. Almost never does a Coach say in a post-match interview, I wasn't good enough this week and I let the team down and I need to improve!

The great Gregor Townsend said, when his Scotland team were defeated in the 2019 Six Nations at home to Ireland, "It was just that final piece, the execution of set-piece which has been really good, that fell off the jigsaw today, and that's my fault. I'm the attack Coach, and we weren't able to get those two or three phases either to get in behind the defence or set up our attack shape.". This rare acceptance of the reason for the loss is something to be admired. It shows the ability to improve and that comes from knowing there is something to improve.

In most instances Coaches like to think that they can show the players how things are to be done. This is evident in the fact that most Coaches wear tracksuits to training and many wear them to matches. There is a frustration in many Coaches that they can't perform the things they want doing, and whilst they are trying so hard to communicate them, they almost always resort to trying to show them. The fact coaches wear tracksuits to training is not a bad thing, it just means they have a more hands-on approach in their communication technique. Verbal communication is so limited and so we use body language daily even if we don't realise we are. Some people are masters of verbal communication, painting accurate pictures and communicating detail clearly. Some are not so articulate, but that doesn't mean they are not good communicators, they just use different communicating tools. As we get older our bodies lose the abilities we had in our younger years, but our brains can go from strength to strength. This means that our ability to demonstrate becomes more limited so it is important we build and learn other communication skills.

The Coach's ability to communicate is the most important skill they will ever hope to have. Getting your own body to perform is hard enough, getting someone else's to... well let's just say that this is where teams are made into great teams.

A Coach must trust in the ability of the player and the player must trust in the knowledge and experience of the Coach. The Coach's ability might have left them many years earlier but the player before them has untapped ability. The Coach must communicate to the player in a way that gets them to understand and trust in the knowledge and experience of the Coach. This is the only way a "wise head on young shoulders" can be achieved. Experience cannot be given it can only be gained. Helping a player to experience for themselves is the Coach's best way of imparting knowledge. In most cases in life someone can explain, until the cows come home, about an experience but there is no true knowledge until the experience is experienced for themselves.

Communication is so important, but communication isn't just for the moment. A Coach's words will be carried onto the field by the team. Whilst the Coaches are sitting in a box high in the stands their words are going round and round inside the heads and hearts of the players. They build strength in the player that is feeling weak, calm in the player that is overwhelmed, focus in the player that is excited and unifies the team to work to the game plan and ultimate success!

Communication isn't just for the moment, sometimes words will stick in your mind for the whole game or even a lifetime.

This understanding of communication brings a lot of responsibility. Just as words can build and strengthen, they can also destroy. There is never an acceptable time when communication should be used in this way. I have seen careers finish before they have begun because a Coach communicated in a way that destroyed rather than built. Frustration can manifest itself in many different ways, but it is something that should be within our control. It only takes a moments frustration that can, if directed in the wrong direction, destroy someone's confidence or belief in themselves. We all have responsibility to not let our communication destroy, just because we couldn't control our frustration. Words can stick in your mind for a lifetime even if they were spoken in just a moment of time.

Think of a Coach's role as a supplier, they must figure out what the team needs and give it to them. Understanding the needs of a team, including each individual player requires great communication skills. Communication is more about listening than it is talking. Coupled with that, most experts agree that communication is between 70-93% nonverbal. This means that a Coach is not just listening to the words of the player but looking at everything they are saying on the pitch. How are they moving? How are they reacting? How are they recovering? How are they? This tells a good Coach far more about a player and team than asking any verbal questions. Likewise, every player will big themselves up to get in the team, however, in almost all circumstances when experts are trying to determine if somebody is lying, the signs are almost always nonverbal. You can't lie about your abilities when you are on the pitch, therefore a good Coach will learn more about a player or team on the training ground or in the game than just talking to them.

This does not mean that verbal communication is not important. Getting a verbal answer and combining it with nonverbal communication will give you the whole picture. An ability to understand a player and team, as well as an understanding of how players and teams view themselves, can give a Coach an understanding of why they are performing in a certain way. There can often be more insight when you are outside looking in. You can't see the wood for the trees and all that! This makes the Coach's job as a communicator so important. Find out what they need and give it to them.

This was demonstrated by Eddie Jones when he took control of the England national team in 2015 after they became the first host nation of a World Cup to go out at the group stage of the tournament. Jones said that the team will feel they let their country down and will try hard to put it right. He said, "My vision was that they should be more 'English', so I kept repeating the message in different ways.". He started to communicate in a way that built the players rather than put them down. Probably the most famous way he changed communication between the Coaches and the Players was with the change of the name "Replacements" to "Finishers". To many, this seemed like a pointless and ridiculous change. The players on the bench had always been there to replace injured or fatigued players to reinforce the team, this did not change with the reclassification to "Finishers", so why make such a seemingly pointless change. Well, this is what the team thought. Hooker, Jamie George, said "We don't ever see ourselves as 'the bench'. Everyone on the bench would love to be starting but we are all of the mindset that we've got to make sure we have an impact on the game. We are the ones who are fresh, we need to lead the team through our voice and actions."

"Replacements" are there in case, however, "Finishers" are there to complete the job. This change in terminology inspired a positive response from each and every player that sits on the bench rather than starting the game. So, when they are called upon to replace a starting player, they see that as a great privilege to be given the responsibility of seeing the game over the line.

England went on to win a record equalling eighteen straight games and Eddie Jones was named World Rugby Coach of the year in 2017. Never has communication been so effectively employed. Now most Rugby teams have "Finishers", not "Replacements".

I was always hopeful of instilling a team mentality in my two boys so, when it came to helping with the chores at home, we put up a rota and gave jobs to them that needed doing. If these jobs were not done on the days that they needed doing I would apply my parental authority and ask them to complete the task or suffer missing out on something. Realising that no matter how often they had to be told they just didn't seem able to remember the next time it needed doing. It was as though it was a chore or something! I realised that they were happy to help but not happy to be given a task. I realised that looking at the rota on the wall was something that reminded them they had to do some housework. To overcome the feeling of dread they had every time they looked at the rota, they just stopped looking at the rota. This meant they continually `forgot` to do their chores and I got tired of having to continually ask them to do them. After a while I realised the constant reminding was not going to change, they were just not interested in looking at the rota. We decided to install some team mentality into doing the housework. On the understanding that they were expecting us to get them to training or games, we explained that we would be doing the housework and it would take us as long as it took. They both, very quickly, realised that when it came to a time for them to go to training, we were still doing housework. It's amazing how much passion a teenager has for housework when they realise that it has to be completed before they can get to a game. This team mentality very quickly made them realise that if they wanted something from the team then they had to contribute to the team. "Dad, can you get me to the game tomorrow"? – "Well, I do have quite a few jobs to do first." – "Ok, what can I do to help?". Suddenly we were communicating with them that the chores needed doing without having to ask.

At work it is easy to put the responsibility of tasks onto others but it is vital for the company that everything runs well and is produced efficiently. Thinking individually about the task will not get it done. As a Coach you must instil a team mentality so if one person is struggling then the team is struggling. If everyone thinks the only way they can succeed is if the team succeeds then they will be ready to provide support without being asked to. They will all be the Finishers with the responsibility to get the job done, get the ball over the line.

I remember when Williams F1 were one of the best Formula 1 teams in the business and were competing for, and winning, World Championships. A guy I worked with knew an engineer at Williams and he had told him that if a driver won a Grand Prix or the Championship then every employee was given a bonus no matter what job they had. Cleaners, Cooks, Admin staff or Pit crew, they were all considered to be part of the team. I am not sure how true that was as the information came to me 3rd hand but in 2015 it was reported that Williams F1 posted a £42.5m loss but 660 staff still received a £3,000 bonus for dedication and hard work.

When it comes to Coaches bringing together a team I have to mention the mastermind that is Jurgen Klopp. I know this is Football, not Rugby, but when he took over at Liverpool FC in 2015 he gathered all the players together in the press room and proceeded to ask every member of staff at the club to walk through one by one. As they passed, he asked the players, "Boys, do you know all of these people? All of these people are here to help you perform at 100%. Do you know their names?". His attitude was that everyone was responsible for the team's success and everyone relied on everyone to be successful, even if you had never kicked a ball. The Cooks are as important as the Striker and the Groundkeeper as important as the Goalkeeper.

This ability for a Coach to cement a team together isn't restricted to the players. Yes, it's the players that score the Try's, make the Tackles, defend the line and win the ball, but it's the team that wins the game. That includes the Nutritionist that decided what each player needs to fuel them through the game, the Kit staff that make sure the kit is present and correct for them to run out onto the pitch feeling ready, the Cleaners who make the changing room, canteens, gyms and rest areas clean and pleasant to be in. The team requires everyone to be at their best to have the best chance of success. If one member of the team does not do their job, the team is not at 100%. It is the Coach's job then to make sure everyone is doing their best for the team as their own success depends on it.

Once the team has been galvanised by a great Coach the game plan needs to be communicated. We have already talked about communication and that the game plan must be understood by all, however, the importance of the game plan itself is not to be underestimated. A great Coach is also a master strategist!

"Thus, it is that the victorious strategist only seeks battle after the victory has been won." The art of war by Sun Tzu.

The game plans that have been employed in the greatest wins, greatest upsets and most controversial games in Rugby history have all been devised by master strategists. The win does not always go to the most superior team. Often the greatest teams do not spend enough time on strategy, as theirs has been working fine, and "if it ain't broke don't fix it"? But for the teams that have not got the skill, power, experience or stamina of many of the greatest teams in the world it doesn't mean that with the right strategist teaching them they can't gain the upper hand.

We saw this in the Six Nations between England and Italy in 2017. The Italians knew they were out classed by England and would easily be turned over by the grand slam holders.

Pundits were expecting England's record score of 80-23 could be bettered on the day. Italy had no chance of winning, or so everybody thought! Italy's Coach Conor O'Shea and his Assistant, England World Cup winner Mike Catt had other ideas. They knew they were outclassed by England, but they didn't want to be humiliated. Their strategy was to take advantage of the way everyone played the game of Rugby. Once a Tackle is made, both teams compete for the ball forming a ruck. Once a ruck is formed an offside line is created across the pitch at the position of the furthest foot back of the players in the ruck. This means that all attacking players must be on their side of the ruck until the ball is played by the opposition. This is how Rugby was, has and is played all around the world. The Italians realised that if they didn't commit to competing for the ball after the tackle then the referee would not be able to call a ruck, and there would be no offside line created. This would leave the Italian's free to stand on England's side of the breakdown without being offside. The first time they did this the crowd erupted, crying for offside. The English team were calling to the Ref to penalise the Italians for offside and Eddie Jones, the best Coach in the business, was furious. The England team were in such disarray they could hardly play the game. England Captain, Dylan Hartley, and Flanker, James Haskell, both veterans of the game were reduced to asking Referee Romain Poite what the rules were. His simple reply was, "I'm the Referee, not a Coach".

The game is won before the game is played, through the hard work put in on the training ground.

So learn to love the process, otherwise it is just hard work!

England were mystified, and although they eventually won the game 36-15, the game is not remembered as an England win, but an Italian strategic wonder, and it was a much closer game than the result suggests. Italy got the result they wanted, not to be humiliated by England but to cause an upset. In fact it was England that looked like a team out played.

We find ourselves frustrated when things don't go as we would like. Strategies, game plans, tactics are all tools in the struggle to win. These tools are picked up through experience, learned and imparted wisdom from veterans of the game. We can all look back on occasions and think we could have done things differently but if we don't learn from them then they become our failures. When we do learn from them, they become our successes of the future! As you go through life write every experience in your strategy book because you can be in no doubt that, even if you don't, someone you know will experience them again. Pull out your strategy book, your book of plays and make a game plan. The greatest Coaches have an ability to get a team to perform far better than their class through good strategies that have taken a lifetime to create.

We all try to tell our kids how to do this or that, or what to expect if they try something new, but did we really listen to our elders when we were young? Building wisdom only comes from education. Living by the words, "every day is a school day", and trying to learn from all experiences, good and bad, can build your book of plays which should constantly be added to. You might not be able to perform anymore but that doesn't mean you can't use the experiences and knowledge you have gathered over the years to still get the win. Watch the great Coaches, they all have notebooks they are scribbling in. Every day they write in their book of plays, building their experience, expanding their knowledge so that when their team is up against the giant in a different class they have the game plan ready to implement. Remember every experience and learn from it so you too can have a book of plays, assured there is something there that can slay the giants and get the win, and above all, when you find yourself in the time of life when you can't do... teach!

There must always be an opposition otherwise there is no game, even if the opposition is friendly, they are still the opposition. Competition is healthy but that does not mean it should be hostile, but sadly in life, it usually is.

We compete in everything, from work to just trying to stand up whilst gravity tries to pull us down. Competition is like training it is crucial in order for us to improve. We have opponents all around us giving us all the competition we need. So why do we complain when some young upstart starts a company in direct competition with us, or someone in the company is after our position. Surely this means, we can play.

The Rugby team always has competition, and they spend time studying the opposition before a game. This is to understand the way they play, their strengths, weaknesses and how they can be beaten. This does not take up their whole training sessions, as the importance of training is to become the best you can be, but it is vitally important you know your opponent. Understanding your opponent means you can prepare yourself for when you meet on the pitch. It is inevitable you will meet when you are in competition with each other.

When you are training and building your team you are always looking for ways to improve and that means understanding past games so you can make your best prediction on the next. We know the past, but we can only make a prediction on the future. That prediction is a guess, but if we understand how we have performed and how our competitors have performed in the past then we can make an educated guess on the future. I am a big believer in looking back to look forward, but very aware that the past only gives you an understanding of what has been, however, that understanding can give you a good sense of what will be.

Understanding how an opposing team has played in the past gives you a good understanding of their strengths and weaknesses. It gives you an understanding of the individual players and how they have performed against their opposite numbers. All players are trying to improve and that means you will always have a different outcome every time a team plays. The result might be win, win, but the way they win will be different every time. This is most notable when a team like the British and Irish Lions go on tour. They tour against a southern hemisphere nation and usually play three games against the national team as well as other teams. These three games never have the same score. These two teams are relatively unchanged throughout the three games but there is always a different outcome. They might win, or even lose, all three games but the games are never the same. This is because the teams are always learning and trying to improve on the weaknesses of the previous game, capitalising on the strengths. That means that even though you are playing against the same players you are not playing the same team. The next game is against a team that knows your weaknesses and understands your strengths. The next game is always against a better team than the last one. If you do not learn and improve you will be beaten, and then beaten again.

Studying the opposition is important to building the right strategy and prepare yourself for the inevitable game, but it must be done in a spirit of improvement. Knowledge of the opposition must be used to build the team so you are not the same team that went into battle in the last game. The opposition is doing the same as you, whether they won or lost, they are learning from the game and making a prediction on how you will play the next. They are preparing themselves for a better `you` by strengthening their weaknesses, building on their strengths and perfecting their strategy based on what they know happened in the past. They are confident they have prepared and are ready to bring their game plan to you.

It is important you understand the opposition is always trying to find your weaknesses and build a team and a game plan to exploit them. There is never a more revealing examination of yourself than through the eyes of your opponent. When we examine ourselves we can be too lenient. Yes, we may be critical of ourselves, but we are usually defensive at the same time. The instinct to protect ourselves usually means we do not take criticism well. We will try to justify ourselves which stops us from improving, choosing to convince ourselves we are right instead. Call it stubborn, call it ignorant, call it whatever you want, we all have a hard time receiving criticism but that needs to change if you are going to improve. You will never get a more honest opinion of your abilities than from someone who wants to beat you, because they are more focused on finding your weaknesses than you are. Listen to the opposition, they can help you far more than your friends who try to be kind. Ok, the opposition might not be willing to sit down and talk to you about your weaknesses, but they will show what they think by their actions. What changes have they made in the team? What are they saying to the media or their supporters? Are they outspoken about particular strengths or are they quiet about certain areas of their team? These might not be obvious signs but if you have an understanding of them as an opponent then their actions can give you some insight as to how they are preparing for the game and, therefore, how they view you as a team!

Be grateful for competition because
there is no game without them, but
don't be hostile.

Thank them for the battle, applaud
them off the pitch and look forward
to the next game.

The opposition will never rest in their desire to beat you. Again, this doesn't mean they are hostile they just want to be the best. This is important for your own development. If you aren't good enough you will lose but you will never know if you are good enough until you come up against opposition. If the opposition aren't trying to beat you then you won't improve because the win will be too easy. In order for Rugby to improve as a sport everyone must want to win and that means wanting to have opponents that want to beat you.

Whether we work for a Company, or run our own business, we must embrace opposition. When there is no competition there is no urgency to improve. If no one is coming to take our job or our customers, why try harder? It's hard to understand the mindset of business owners when new technology or competition comes along and takes their business from them. They feel cheated and entitled to stay in business simply because they have been in business for a long time. With modern technology evolving so fast things that were done five years ago, let alone fifty years ago, are being done more efficiently, effectively and affordably. That means any Company or employee who is not prepared to learn, improve and adapt to the new game will find themselves taken off the field, no longer able to compete with the new teams.

Embrace competition and learn from it, it will teach you more about yourself than anything else. This is the ultimate in training techniques, find out where you are weak and strengthen. Find out what you are up against and adapt. Find out who your opposition is and understand their strengths, weaknesses and build a game plan to win.

When you win, you will inevitably have to play the opposition again, and if you have not improved you can be sure they have! That could be the difference between success and failure.

Winning or losing is not the result. What happens to the team and players because of the win or loss is the result. If it makes you stronger then it is a win, even if you were defeated. If you are left unimproved, or even retrograde, then it is a loss even if you were triumphant. When we win, we celebrate, when we lose we deliberate.

Steve Hansen gave credit to the New Zealand selectors for keeping faith in the Coaching trio of Graham Henry, Wayne Smith and himself after the All Blacks` disastrous Quarter-Final loss to France at the 2007 World Cup. The three Coaches, some say controversially, had their contracts extended from 2009 to the end of the next World Cup in 2011. "You have got to remember we bombed the World Cup in 2007" Hansen said. "We were the best team by far going into that tournament and we bombed it by not understanding what World Cups are about."

Giving Henry and his team the opportunity to learn the lessons of defeat and continue to develop and build the All Blacks` team is not very common in modern elite sports.

There seems to be a trend in replacing the Coaches when the team has underperformed. It's understandable given a realistic timeframe. If a Coach cannot get a team to perform consistently then there has to be a time when change is made. This realistic timeframe, however, often doesn't seem very realistic at all, just take a look at the English Football leagues. This is often driven by the impatience of the supporters, but I would not say this is their fault. So much promise and expectation is heaped onto the incoming Manager that they either make an immediate impression or they are seen to be letting the club down. Some supporters were even calling for Sir Alex Ferguson to be fired in his early years at Manchester United because of inconsistent results. He went on to be the most successful Manager in English football history.

Graham Henry, Wayne Smith and Steve Hanson went on to win the 2011 World Cup. Steve Hanson was promoted to Head Coach of the infamous All Blacks side as Henry stepped down, and he went on to victory in the very next World Cup in 2015. Hanson ended his time in charge of the All Blacks after the 2019 World Cup in Japan with a record ninety three wins, four draws and just ten losses and became the greatest All Blacks Coach in their history and one of the greatest Coaches in the world!

It is also worth mentioning that the Captain of that losing team against France in 2007 became one of the greatest All

Blacks of all time, the legend that is Richie McCaw. Winning the next two consecutive World Cups as Captain, he went on to become the most capped Test Rugby player of all time until Alun Wyn Jones superseded him. He also won the World Rugby Player of The Year Award three times and was eventually named World Rugby Player of The Decade.

A defeat is never defining of a team. Often amazing teams will lose to lowly opponents. They get berated and criticised, but they are always expected to be better. This is not usually the case in real life. We are judged only to be as good as our last performance. We lose our job's, miss out on promotions or even lose friendships without being given the opportunity to improve. This is never more apparent than the way we look at school grades. The grade isn't education, the grade is how well we did in the moment, however, these grades can define our lives.

Never has anyone been judged more for a performance than, it seems, we do with our children's examination grades. Colleges judge them on their school results, Universities judge them on their College results and then Employers judge them on their University results. Rarely ever do we forget the result and look at their abilities and potential. I know there are many of you saying, "we always look for potential in our next employee." That may be true but when was the last time you employed someone who had terrible or no educational results but decided they were right for the position anyway. Do your own examination of someone because we are all different. Their last performance may have been the only one they didn't do well in. The Media always covers results day to see the look on the faces of the students and report on whether grades were up or down this year. What becomes apparent is that the one piece of education these young people are missing is how to lose. There is so much pressure to get the result that gives them the opportunity to go to the right College or School to get offered a position in their chosen University. They seem unprepared for anything other than success.

In Rugby clubs around the world there is a culture of development on and off the pitch. It doesn't matter if you are not planning on becoming the next Maggie Alphonsi or Jonathan Joseph there is a foundation of respect, teamwork, support and development to help each other when you are knocked down to get back up and be stronger for it. Surely the education system today can learn so much from the principles of Rugby. Sometimes you lose, so improve and go again.

When my sons were at school, I tried to give them the understanding that a result is not defining of them. They both did well at school, but I wanted them to understand that working hard and giving your all will lead to success, and that working hard and giving your all will continue long after results day. They both have different abilities and academic strengths and weaknesses, but not giving themselves extra pressure to get a particular grade gave them the ability to focus on, and enjoy, every step of their development and to love the process. According to Steve Hanson, Richie McCaw was not their most talented player but what he did have was a work ethic to keep striving to be the best. Hanson said although McCaw wasn't the most talented, he was their greatest player by far. Focus on the process not the result because without a strong work ethic there are no results.. Enjoy the process and the results will be what they are. You must love the process otherwise it is just really hard work.

Rugby players love training, playing, developing and improving. This is the process that leads to success. Although they love to win, they also love to play when they lose. This doesn't mean they like losing, this means they love the process. The process is what makes them improve, become more intelligent, stronger, more agile and more unified as a team. The process is what makes them a Rugby player. If they win, they want to play again. If they lose, they really want to play again. They love the process and that means they get the results without thinking about the results.

This is the same for all of us, even those of us that say we don't care if we win or lose. Life is competitive every day. Our bodies are competing against viruses and bacterial infections at this very moment. Our desires and lusts are contesting our will power and we are all working hard to get the best wage or the right results. Everyone is competing in one way or another!

When my son went to collect his exam results, he said he couldn't believe how stressed everyone was. Some of his friends were in tears and his mates were asking him if he was nervous. He replied, "why would I be nervous? There is nothing I can do now. I worked hard and did everything I could, and the results will be what they are. I will have to work with what I get knowing it's the best I could have done." He did very well, and I was proud of him!

I left school with barely any qualifications. I didn't care, because I put myself in a position where I didn't need them. I limited my potential and entered a career that didn't rely on my grades, I limited myself. I have never been asked for my grades because I haven't put myself in the position that required it. This is not the way to do it though!

I started in the Construction industry as an Apprentice and I worked at it like I needed to be the best Apprentice there had ever been. I didn't like employment because my employers weren't as devoted as me and that meant my enthusiasm turned to frustration. I couldn't get the Company to do better because my employer didn't want to work at it. This frustration drove me to start my own Company and, although it was very small I could drive it. Soon after starting my own Company I realised that I was a Director with no qualifications doing what my "grade A" peers hadn't done. I then understood that I was my only limitation, not my grades.

Not giving children an understanding of competition and subsequent loss whilst they are at school does not give them the vital understanding of how to deal with loss when they have to stand on their own two feet.

We have created the situation where our kids are pinning all their hopes on their grades and, if they don't get what they are expecting, they don't know what to do. There is always more than one way to get to where you want to be, as long as we learn from the loss and are better for it.

There was once a young boy that loved to play Rugby, and like all young players, he wanted to be the best. He played for his school, and local club, but no matter how good he was, he never got picked for any regional academies or national youth sides. He left school at 16 and started a career as a trainee scaffolder. He continued to play Rugby for his local amateur club and, more importantly, continued to better himself as a player and person. Not focusing on having been overlooked during his younger playing days, he focused on becoming the best Rugby player he could be. When he was 20 years old, he was playing for his club when the Head Coach of Llanelli, Anthony Buchanan, came to watch the game. Buchanan was so impressed he invited the 20-year-old to Llanelli. Just 3 years later he won the Welsh Professional Players Association 'Welsh Player of the Year'. To cut a long story short, that young boy has now won the Guinness PRO12 title with Scarlets, the Gallagher Premiership title and Heineken Champions Cup with Saracens and a 6 Nations Grand Slam with Wales. He was selected for the British and Irish Lions tour to New Zealand in 2017 and has been capped 68 times for his country. That determined young boy is Liam Williams. Just because things don't happen the way you planned, doesn't mean they can't still happen. There is always another way.

The result might not be defining of a Rugby player, however, they never go out onto the pitch to lose. They might go out expecting to lose because the opposition is a different class, but they still go out to try and win. Even when a team is in a competition where they do not need to put their strongest side on the pitch for a particular game, the reserve and youth players go out with the team with one desire in mind, to win!

We might criticise when a team loses but we still understand their abilities and never change our view of their potential. At work we are often judged on our last performance, never on how much we can improve, and the next guy is tapping us on the shoulder, waiting, ready to step into our shoes. We heap pressure on ourselves and our employees to get it right first time and then the process becomes a struggle rather than an enjoyment. We need to learn to enjoy the process, and if we are not then something needs to change.

A loss is often a better result than a win.

Losing is learning and will often lead to greater success.

When we win we celebrate, when we lose we deliberate!

If you are an employer, try to find out what makes your staff tick and offer a solution for them to enjoy their job, you will find they are far more productive for it. It sounds far more simple than it is but if you love what you do, you do it well. Likewise, if you are employed and you don't love your job, either find a way to make it enjoyable or find another job that you can enjoy. We all spend too much time at work to not be enjoying it.

I understand how difficult it is to be in a job you are not motivated in or enjoying. It can seem impossible to see a way out and that we just don't have a choice, stuck in a dead- end job. You may not be in control of the job or your employer but you are in control of you, so you can decide if you are positive or negative and that will determine how your day was.

If you are positive not only will your work day be more positive but all aspects of your life will become more positive. Once you start to feel positive in all aspects of your life, things don't seem so difficult anymore. Suddenly work isn't such a pain and you come home more refreshed and energetic. Being more refreshed and energetic at home gives you more energy at work and therefore it feels easier.

Once you have positivity flowing through all areas of your life you will become more attractive and more opportunities will present themselves to you. Employers will see you as energetic and self-motivated and will either want to employ or promote you, and suddenly, changing your career may not seem so difficult. Family and friends will feel refreshed and energised around you.

Positivity is infectious and can have an astonishing effect on your life, however negativity can be equally devastating. Just try being more positive about your situation and then see how easy it is to do something you enjoy every day!

When it comes to learning from defeat, they don't get much more famous than the greatest basketball player of all time Michael Jordan. He said, "I've missed more than 9000 shots in my career, I've lost almost 300 games. 26 times I have been trusted to take the game winning shot and missed. I've failed over and over again in my life, and that is why I succeed".

Babe Ruth is in the Baseball Hall of Fame after setting many records and reportedly making 714 career home runs, however, alongside his home runs another record of 1,330 strikeouts. In 1923 he broke the record for the most home runs in a season, also the record for highest batting average. He was struck out more times than any other player in Major League Baseball that same year. He famously said, "Never let the fear of striking out keep you from playing the game. Every strike brings me closer to the next home run."

Even when you think you keep getting beaten, just remember you can't beat the person who never gives up!

Without the loss in 2007 I wonder if Richie McCaw would have become the Greatest player of the decade?

I think I need to start with the wording at the end of this chapter...

"If you are the greatest you can be, you are a champion! "

That sounds a bit cheesy when put straight out there but at the end of the day we all want to be happy. Unless we are fulfilled we are not truly satisfied and therefore not truly happy. To enable us to fulfil our potential we must become the greatest we can be in whatever it is we want to be. Some of us may be happy in our misery, but happy none the less. Everyone has their own concept of what that is, but we still all want happiness.

The Champion is the greatest of all, the mightiest who cannot be beaten. They work hard and are devoted to their craft with a 'never give up' attitude. They eat, sleep and breathe it until they become the Champions. Everyone is trying to become the Champion, so why then, do some become Champions and others don't? Some say it's talent, genetics, God given ability and skill, genius even. I'm sure all these things have something to do with it, except for the ones you have never heard of. The ones that had all the above but didn't play. They had other commitments, other passions, didn't know it was a possibility or just wanted to spend their time doing something else instead. So many through the ages

126

who could have become the greatest, but for one reason or the other just didn't. It's always staggered me how many people you speak to who say they could have been a sporting this or that but, for an injury, had commitments or they were not given the chance. Excuses and laziness are one thing but there are also many out there that never knew they could have been the greatest or just plain didn't want to be. This makes the ones that do become Champions, a select group, and different to everyone else. Ok, you may say not everyone has the physical ability to become a Rugby player, and yes, there is a part that the gene plays but that doesn't stop you having a go. I know for a fact that if anyone practices at something they can improve. Emmitt Smith, three times Super Bowl Winner said, "All men are created equal, just some of us worked harder in pre-season."

The mindset of the Champion is an obsession to be the best. They are determined to improve because they know that if they don't improve the next guy will. That obsessive mindset was what made Sarah Hunter the world's best!

The MMA champion Conor McGregor said, "There's no talent here, this is hard work. This is an obsession."

Every Rugby player knows that to become a Champion you have got to be obsessed. The definition of obsession is the state in which a person's mind is completely filled with thoughts of one particular thing that there is no capacity for anything else. This means that those who become

Champions are focused on becoming the best they can be and nothing else. This is the difference between those that are good and those that become Champions.

Most Champions aren't interested in proving to the world they are the greatest, they are only interested in becoming the best they can be for themselves. We have seen the resulting fame and fortune many of these Megastars receive, however, they know that results do not define the Rugby player.

A Rugby player does not go to training to win trophies and awards, they go to training to become the best they can be. If the trophies and awards come along then great but the mindset is all about improving and becoming the best you can be. This obsession to be the best is not just about improving the player individually it's about improving the team. The player strives to be the best, that includes integrating into the team and improving their teammates at the same time. There is no real point in improving yourself if you are not working to improve the team at the same time. You strive to be the best so that you can add value to the team, and when the team is striving to become the greatest you all gain in value. This mindset makes Champions! The same mindset in the Coaches, Physio, Nutritionist, and club staff creates an obsession to become the greatest that is infectious and will only bring great success.

If you play to win a game, you need to be better than the opposition. But if you play to become Champions you need to be better than you were yesterday.

When this obsession is in the heart of the team there is harmony, everyone working to the same goal, to be the best! There is no misunderstanding, infighting or lack of effort. Everyone is working to be the best they can be because they know that is the only way the team can become the best it can be. Because of this desire to be the best they can't help but improve.

This desire to be the best brings coherence and coordination to the team or, in other words, harmony. Everyone working together in harmony means that the team is as good as it can be. Going into a game with a state of harmony means there are no weaknesses for the opposition to exploit. The team can be confident it has prepared and finds strength in its combined belief that it is the best. This is the first thing the opposition will have to face.

During the 2019 world cup, England came up against the All Blacks in the semi-final. New Zealand performed their Haka, which is a show of strength. It is to show the opposition their pride, strength and unity. In most cases the opposition stands in front of the New Zealand team and tries not to be intimidated by them. However, it is such an intimidating display with each player locking eyes on an opposing player, it's hard not to be influenced by it. On this occasion the

129

England team, led by Owen Farrell, formed an inverted V towards the All Blacks, like a giant mouth opened to swallow them up. As the cameras realised what was happening, they panned out to show the spectacle in full. The crowds erupted, and even those who were watching on the TV went wild with excitement. Hair stood up on the back of every England supporters' neck when the cameras focused in onto Farrells face. With a knowing smile that said, "you can try, but you won't beat us"! He stood defiant, confident and full of belief in his team. I have seen many teams try and get the better of the All Blacks during the Haka, but this is the only time I have seen it done successfully. England looked like the team with all the pride, strength and unity. England looked like the team with all the confidence and belief. England looked intimidating!

The England team won the display of unity and then won the game, beating New Zealand 19-7 in one of their greatest performances. The result was already written all over Owen Farrell's face before the first ball had been kicked. This knowledge that you have become the greatest you can be is what wins the game.

This obsession to be the best you can be must continue, until you can't continue any more. England learned this the hard way in the final. After showing they were the Champions against New Zealand they went into the final against South Africa as clear favourites. However, they turned up to the game late. With half an hour to go before kick-off, England hadn't even started a proper warm up. The players seemed disconnected, and as they ran out onto the pitch for kick off, Owen Farrells face did not have that same confident look. His smile seemed almost forced. The England team didn't look like the harmonious team they had done just one week before. Their now trademark, quick well drilled start, was not there. South Africa had the kick-off and were straight up onto England. Ben Youngs took the ball at the back of the ruck for a box kick but there were no Forwards to give him protection. After having to beckon in Kyle Sinckler twice, to give him protection to box kick, South Africa had all the time to setup to receive the high kick. South Africa took the high ball and one phase later Courtney Lawes` attempted Tackle found himself on the wrong side of the ruck, pinned down by the South African Forwards and he was penalised for not rolling away. Not even a minute of the game had passed, and it was apparent England were not the well drilled team they had been and they were lucky not to be three points down.

Within three minutes of play England kicked away possession again and, as South Africa attacked, Kyle Sinckler and Maro Itoje collided in the Tackle resulting in Sinckler being knocked unconscious, having to be replaced. Although this was an unfortunate injury it just seemed to show again that England were nothing like the harmonious team who beat the All Blacks and now their confidence was knocked by losing a key player. South Africa had shown how fast and hard they were, and England didn't seem able to respond. Every time England kicked the ball down the field South Africa came back with speed, power, and precision. England couldn't even pass an accurate ball, missing their targets and adding to the pressure they were under, playing themselves into trouble until they gave away penalties. South Africa, on the other hand, were quicker to the high balls, quicker to the breakdowns and more accurate passing and tackling. They were more powerful overall and looked like the Champions from the kick-off. South Africa went on to victory and equalled New Zealand's record of three world cup victories.

England were a victim of their own success. It seemed that they were more interested in the result than in being the best. There was so much hype about England that there was already talk about an open bus tour when they returned with the trophy. Although the England team said they were focused on the game, the game said otherwise. South Africa on the other hand, who had been written off, were outstanding. South Africa were well drilled, prepared and focused. They were the best they could be, and that's why they were the Champions.

Being the best you can be, is a constant process. Even if England had been as good as they were against New Zealand they may still have been beaten by South Africa, but they would have returned home as heroes. The fact they were not as good as they could have been is what let them down.

South Africa were outstanding, and I am certainly not taking away from their achievements, but to understand why some are Champions and others aren't, is to realise that striving to be your best is constant. Everyone is striving to be the Champions but those that become Champions are the ones that always strive to improve, even when they are the best.

Becoming your best is not simply about setting goals and achieving them. Goals are important but anyone can set a goal and achieve it, just don't set very hard goals. This isn't the same as being your best. Pushing yourself to becoming your best requires improvement day after day and that means setting goals that are just out of your reach, and if you reach that goal, set a harder one. Many people give in to the daily struggle, admitting to themselves that they couldn't do this or that. This is because it's easier to say something is impossible than it is to prove it can be done. We are all different and some of us have different abilities and skills, including different physical attributes. Some might be tall and strong and suited to playing in the second row. Others might be shorter, quick, nimble and suited to playing as a Full Back. These different physical attributes might be better suited to different ways of playing but if a Prop had their heart set on becoming a Winger, they may not become world class, but with hard work and determination, they could improve to become the best Winger they could be. How good `the best you can be` is, will not be known until you have achieved it, and when you achieve it is up to you. The Champion may be called the greatest, but they never believe they are the best they can be. Listen to any Champion and they will always say they can improve.

The result does not define you, being the best you can be defines you, and it will give you fulfilment and therefore happiness, and that's the ultimate success. Happiness is the goal everyone strives for, it's just that most of us don't realise it's within ourselves to get it. Nothing external can give you happiness. Yes, you can feel pleasure from external sources but these are always finite and will never give you fulfilment. So many times, we try to gain something external, thinking it will give us that happiness we are craving or needing. We spend billions on things, or stuff that we feel will complete us or show to the world we have success, just to feel as empty the next day. Being the best you can be is the only way you will feel fulfilment.

Striving to be the best you can be, whether that's in business or your personal life, means if you mess up or make a mistake you will be better for it. You will learn from your experiences and feel more fulfilled every day. We all mess up but, in trying to improve every day, you will always be the best you can be. You might not be as good as the next guy that is trying to take your customers but, if they are better than you, that's fair play. As long as you were as good as you could be then, and keep improving every day, you will be happy about it. The trouble comes when you don't do your best and the next guy takes your customers. You are then plagued with disappointment that you could have changed the outcome. You could have stopped it. You had the ability, but didn't.

Every player wants to be on the field. A Rugby player lives to play the game, they would play for nothing other than the pleasure of it, and just as passionately. That said, they all feel they can have an influence on the game whether by starting or finishing, as long as they get on the field. You can see it in the eyes of the players that come onto the pitch from the bench when the team is trailing. They run onto the pitch like they are about to turn it all around, slapping their teammates on the shoulders to rouse them and giving over commands from the Coaches on how to change the game for the better. They believe they can win by influencing their teammates to up their game. They believe, with all their being, they are going to win because they have been given the opportunity to go out and win it. It is true you can't win a game if you are not involved, and if you want to be on the pitch you have to be at your best. Therefore, if you strive to be your best you will have a chance of being on the pitch and if you are on the pitch then you have a chance of winning the game, and if you keep winning, then you will be Champions.

Improve and be your best every day! Encourage your team, whether at home, school, work or socially, to be their best and you will only ever experience success. You will be fulfilled, satisfied and truly happy.

If you are the greatest you can be, you are a Champion!

Ok! Why Rugby? Why play? Why be a spectator? Why title the last chapter "Why"? Why read or write this book? Why have a business? Why work for this company? Why? Why? Why?

When it comes to the question "why", we have some weird inhibitions. Kids on the other hand, don't! They are relentless with the `W` bomb, tear your hair out relentless. When did we develop this reservation to question everything? The biggest limitation on us all is the answer, "because that's the way it's done." This stops us considering any change and therefore stunts growth, innovation, creativity and development.

We have seen how the Rugby Union game has changed over the years and this applies to all sports. As sports have gained in popularity, so the competition has increased. This means if you want to become the best you have got to work harder. This means the way things were done had to be questioned.

Once the Winger was a nimble, light weight, agile and speedy player but someone decided to ask the question `why`? Why wouldn't you put a 6'5" 18.5 stone Flanker on the Wing? They wouldn't have to be the fastest or most agile because they would have the strength, weight and power to run through their opposite number. Enter Jonah Lomu, he was built like a Flanker and played as a Flanker, until someone asked "why"? and didn't accept, "because that's the way it's played". When Lomu played on the Wing all eyes were on him. No one had seen anything like him before. He was not just strength and power, he had speed too. This combination was devastating on the Wing, running through his opponents, it usually took three or four men to bring him down. He was one of the first purpose-built Rugby players. Rugby Union used to be an amateur sport and back then none of our Rugby heroes were professional, they all had other jobs. This meant that although they were great Rugby players of their generation, they were all having to split their time between Rugby and their jobs. In 1995 Rugby Union became a professional sport and gave players the opportunity to give 100% of their time to the game, meaning the Rugby player was now able to become a full-time athlete. Jonah Lomu became an icon of the 90's, he was a new breed of Rugby player, a true athlete built solely for Rugby. He retired from international Rugby in 2002 and from the professional game in 2007. During his time in Rugby, the Rugby player got bigger, stronger, faster, more skilful and much more technical. The world had to respond to Jonah Lomu or be left behind. If you stick with what is winning today, you will lose tomorrow.

Jonah Lomu is probably the reason half the supporters in the 90's became Rugby supporters. He didn't just change position he changed the game. It is thanks to Jonah Lomu for questioning the game that made Rugby the spectacle it is today.

I think there is a real insecurity around things we don't know or understand. Now I am "middle aged" I can understand this feeling of insecurity. There are many things in the world of social media I don't understand, from emojis to Tik Tok. It is an alien world to many of us, but it is the new world. The next generation will be amazed that there was once a time when we didn't communicate with symbols or bizarre abbreviations. In ten years-time it will be commonplace to have a business meeting with people that learned how to communicate via Snapchat, and for those of us who don't know what that is we will have a lot of catching up to do.

What I do understand is that with the internet making the knowledge of the world so readily available, everyone is an expert. Today we ask Google, and the hard work is done for us. We are experts at anything we want to be because the knowledge is in our pockets.

This knowledge in our pockets means that the world is moving in two directions, those that are learning from others and those that are leaving the learning to others. Those that are learning from others are like the Forwards being lifted in the lineout, reaching further because of the work put in by others. Those that are leaving the learning to others, however, are becoming more and more influenced by others. The internet is amazing, giving us access to knowledge that we would never have had access to before, but so many of us are not taking the opportunity to improve. We must adapt to this new world of fast innovation.

If you are like me and lived a life when a phone was attached to a wall and only used if you wanted to speak to someone more than 2 miles away. Look back on those days with fond memories but to continue to be successful you will need to adapt or you will be overtaken. If you stick with what is winning today you will lose tomorrow!

Mental preparation is so important in developing a Rugby player, learning every day, otherwise they are left behind. Learning about the game, yourself, your team and your opposition is vital to improve and develop. It has been shown in many studies that learning a new skill improves focus and mental efficiency. When we are learning how to do something new our brains respond by building synaptic connections between neurons in the brain. This growth not only gives us an ability to achieve what we are learning to do, but it also gives us an ability to learn similar skills making it easier and quicker for us to develop. Research has also linked stimulating the brain to learn new skills with a lower risk of memory problems and illnesses. Learning every day is the same as exercising your body. Everyone is well aware what happens when we don't exercise, there is a physical manifestation. We lose muscle and start to store the energy we get from food as fat. We start to lack energy, and this makes it harder to motivate ourselves to exercise, adding to the problem. The same happens to our brain, if we don't exercise it, however, we don't see the physical manifestation so easily. Just as our bodies need exercise to keep going our brains need the same. The world is changing at an amazing rate and if we want to keep up, let alone stay ahead of the game, then we need to keep learning.

Why is learning considered something we did in our youth, when we were 'students', rather than a daily pastime? If a Rugby player has learned how to play their position and has the necessary skills to compete, why do they continue going to training? Surely the veterans of the game would just turn up for the game on the weekend and do nothing more? Our mentality is to learn how to fulfil the position we want to be employed as, then just turn up and do the job. Perhaps this is why so many of us feel we are stuck in a dead-end job! The Rugby player knows that learning new skills, or how to improve and develop themselves, is the only way to continue at the level they are playing because every other player will get better and better leaving them behind. In Rugby you often find that the veterans are the first to training, ready to improve and develop. They seem more eager and determined to work hard in training than the young new players. This is because they have had the experience of seeing what happens if you don't improve.

Spending time thinking the way I do about Rugby has given me more understanding of how we integrate and operate within a personal and professional community. As most of us enjoy sports, and therefore understand the sports team, we are almost there. My girlfriend played Netball in school, my Dad played cricket, a friend played football and I played Rugby. None of us played to any sort of high level and only recreationally but we all understand the sport and its team mentality. Even friends of mine who do not play sports, but enjoy watching a sport, understand sport and its` team mentality.

So why Rugby? Rugby is an amazing game that can be enjoyed by anyone at any level of experience. You don't have to be a scholar to enjoy the excitement, power and skill of the game. I am aware that everyone is different, and some people don't enjoy Rugby. You are in control of you and how you are influenced by others so if you have a love for another sport just look at how they work and you will see the same principles. Whether its Rugby Union or League, Netball, Volleyball, Football, Cricket, Basketball, Baseball, Golf, Boxing, Athletics, Tennis, Lacrosse, Curling, the list is endless. If you have a sport you are part of, or have a passion for, just see for yourself. The way to work in a team and be successful is right there in front of you. You already know it just apply the way they work to your life and you will have a winning team mentality in no time.

Life doesn't go the way we expect, it bobbles and bounces and is difficult to grasp hold of. The world is not perfectly round and seems very odd at times. It certainly doesn't help that everyone seems to be trying to outdo you, put you down, stamp all over you and leave you face down in the dirt. I have found that understanding Rugby has given me some answers to life's odd ways, such as:

- You are different to the rest of your team, but that means you fit in, so embrace it.
- Losing is learning and is also inevitable, so learn to lose and appreciate it.
- Be grateful for the competition because there is no game without them, don't be hostile, thank them for the battle and look forward to the next one.
- Learn from the hard work of those that have gone before, give your knowledge to the next, and you will reach higher than you could ever imagine.
- Give support where it's wanted but be careful not to interfere where you are not needed.
- Chase every opportunity because you never know how it is going to bounce. Put in the hard work and prepare, so when it does pop up you can grasp it with both hands and go for the Try line.
- A great leader works for their team and therefore the team follow their leader.
- Only once the game is won on the training ground do you go into battle, so learn to love the process.

- And, if you can't do, teach!

Above all these principles is Respect! First and foremost, Rugby is a game of respect!

Respect your team, respect your opposition, respect your supporters, respect the Ref, respect Rugby and Respect yourself!

Respect is the lubricant that keeps the world turning. Without respect there is no society, no safety, no cooperation, no development and no love. The world needs respect in order to keep turning. Rugby is built on respect like no other sport. Players do battle, draw blood, batter, bruise and break each other and then, when the game is over, they applaud each other off the pitch.

My son was already feeling that Rugby was giving him a good understanding of the world around him when he was offered a place in the London Irish Development Player Program. He was looking forward to developing his Rugby abilities but the thing that helped him more than anything was their motto, `Positive Passionate Relentless Discipline`.

Using Rugby to understand teamwork, leadership, personal development and a positive mindset is why, for me, Rugby is life!

Rugby is a game of intelligence, strategy, teamwork and mental and physical strength. These are the principles a Rugby player needs to develop in order to succeed in the game.

Get out there and win it!